EXPLORING ST HELENA:
A WALKER'S GUIDE

Ian Mathieson and Laurence Carter

Exploring St Helena: A Walker's Guide

ANTHONY NELSON

First published by Anthony Nelson Ltd
PO Box 9, Oswestry, Shropshire SY11 1BY, England
on behalf of The St Helena Government

ISBN 0 904614 49 2

Designed by Alan Bartram
Typeset by Nene Phototypesetters Ltd, Northampton
Printed in England by The Bath Press, Avon

Contents

Acknowledgements 6
Introduction 9

A Walk around Jamestown 11

Coastal walks 15

1 Breakneck Valley 16
2 Mundens – Sampsons Battery – Jamestown 17
3 Deadwood – Pipe Path – Ruperts 20
4 Flagstaff Hill – Banks Battery – Ruperts 22
5 Flagstaff Hill – Knotty Ridge – The Barn 25
6 Turks Cap Valley 27
7 Prosperous Bay 29
8 Sharks Valley 31
9 Bellstone – Great Stone Top 33
10 Rose Rock – Powell's Valley – Green Hill 35
11 Green Hill – Sandy Bay Barn 37
12 Sandy Bay Beach – Lot's Wife Ponds 39
12a Sandy Bay Beach – Potato Bay 41
13 Botleys – Manati Bay 43
14 Thompson's Valley 44
15 Sarah's Valley – Lemon Valley 46

Inland walks 49

16 Briars – Barnes Road – Francis Plain 50
17 Oakbank – Bates Branch – White Gate 52
18 Casons Gate – Farm Buildings – Casons Gate 54
19 Casons – Broad Bottom – Thompson's Hill – Casons 56
20 Ball Alley – Blue Point – Old Lufkins 58
21 Old Lufkins – Fairyland – Bamboo Hedge 60
22 Halley's Mount – The Peaks – Teutonic 62
23 Cabbage Tree Road – The Peaks – Wranghams 64
24 Teutonic – Pleasant Valley – Silver Hill 66
25 Longwood Gate – Fisher's Valley – Longwood Gate 68

26 **Other walks (and Points of Interest)** 71

(A) ON THE COAST 71
Deep Valley, Prosperous Signal Station, Dry Gut, Broad Gut, Man and Horse, Goat Pound Ridge, Egg Island

(B) INLAND 72
Thompson's Wood, Horse Pasture, Half Moon, Willowbank, Rock Rose, High Hill, High Peak, Heart Shape Waterfall, Diana's Peak Ring Road, Napoleon's Tomb, Sane Valley, Plantation Forest, High Knoll, Knollcombes, West Lodge

References and Recommended Reading 76

Index 77

Acknowledgements

The idea for this book developed during 1989 when the authors were involved with the project to update St Helena's maps. The island's history and geography is reflected on the maps but the user is left wondering about many of the romantic place names and the dramatic array of features portrayed. The final decision to write the book was taken during one of the least exciting walks to Bencoolen in early 1990. The idea was not original; indeed a walks book was produced as a typescript in the 1960s (by Talbot-Phibbs). However copies of this cannot be easily obtained today and many of the walks have changed.

Our thanks are due to all those who provided suggestions and contributions including Neil McCulloch for his ornithological notes, John Bailey, Nicholas Thorpe, Trevor Hearl and Basil George for comments on the text and other assistance. Thanks also to Dave Bentham, who took some of the photographs, and to Tony Nelson for producing the book. We are also grateful to the Saints who showed us many of the paths, and who helped to make our stay on the island so enjoyable.

For financial help and advice we wish to acknowledge the combined assistance of UNESCO, ODA and the St Helena Government. Support has also been provided by the Education Department and Curnow Shipping and administrative assistance by the Secretariat. Thanks are due to Kew Gardens for permission to publish extracts from the Burchell collection: see References and Recommended Reading. Maps have been reproduced with the permission of the Ordnance Survey who retain the copyright.

Finally we wish to thank our wives and children and many others who have continued to keep St Helena and her walks alive for us since we left the island.

'We go ashore.' (Graphic 1886)

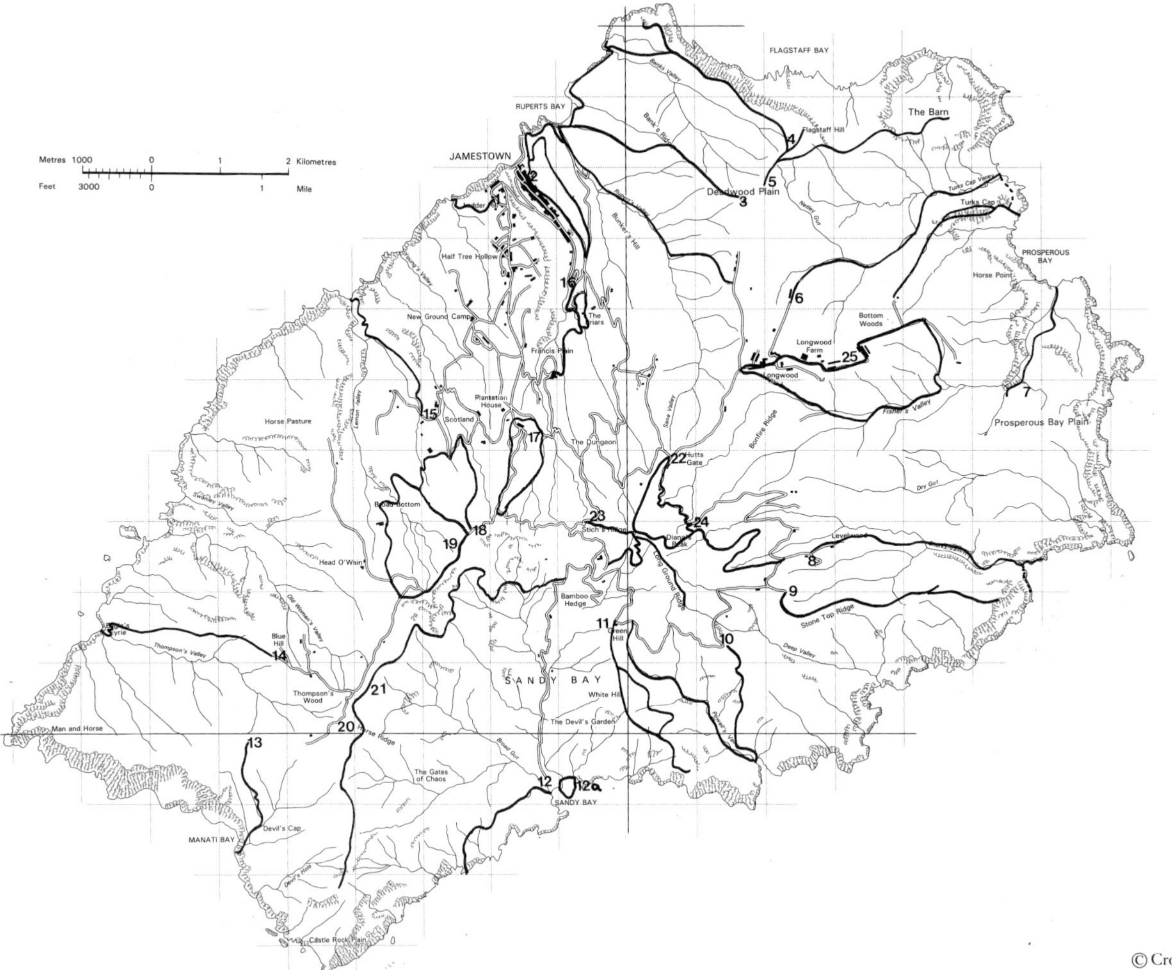
FLAGSTAFF BAY
RUPERTS BAY
JAMESTOWN
Metres 1000 0 1 2 Kilometres
Feet 3000 0 1 Mile
The Barn
Flagstaff Hill
Deadwood Plain
Turks Cap Valley
Turks Cap
PROSPEROUS BAY
Horse Point
Half Tree Hollow
New Ground Camp
Bottom Woods
Longwood Farm
Longwood
Francis Plain
Plantation House
Scotland
Horse Pasture
Fisher's Valley
Prosperous Bay Plain
The Dungeon
Hutts Gate
Broad Bottom
Stich's Ridge
Dry Gut
Levelwood
Head O'Wain
Bamboo Hedge
Stone Top Ridge
Blue Hill
Thompson's Valley
Green Hill
Deep Valley
SANDY BAY
White Hill
Thompson's Wood
The Devil's Garden
Man and Horse
Horse Ridge
Broad Gut
The Gates of Chaos
SANDY BAY
MANATI BAY
Devil's Cap
Devil's Hole
Castle Rock Plain
© Crown Copyright

Introduction

Despite 1,400 cars and nearly 100 kilometres of road, much of St Helena can be seen only on foot. The island has a surprising effect, converting people who have never been keen on walking into intrepid explorers who tackle the routes to the Barn or Sharks Valley with gay abandon. Part of the reason must be St Helena's spectacular and varied landscape, which allows a traverse to be made from desert to green pasture in the course of an afternoon. The terrain hosts a unique flora, whose remnants can be found all over the island, and also the endemic wirebird. But above all there can be few islands whose past offers such a great and abiding interest. While much of St Helena's history is associated with better-known places such as Jamestown, Longwood House and Plantation, a significant part is more diffuse and lies in the scattered ruins and evocative place names that reflect the early years of habitation and the island's important strategic role.

Twenty-five main walks are described in this book. A section at the end gives a brief description of a number of shorter routes and places of interest, but the book begins in the capital, since this is every visitor's first view of the island. Each walk description includes items of history and natural history that might be of interest along the way. The majority of 'things to see' on St Helena are covered – apart from details of Plantation House and Napoleon's residences, which are topics in their own right. A little basic knowledge of St Helena's history adds to the enjoyment of many of the anecdotes related in the course of the walks; the fullest history is that by Gosse, but Tony Cross's book provides a good précis (see Recommended Reading for details of these and other books containing good background information).

Extracts from the current Ordnance Survey maps indicate the routes of the walks. However, since the precise course of a route is not always clear, even on the ground, the maps cannot be treated as totally accurate, and it is always best to walk a new route with someone who knows the way.

Especial care is needed on some of the walks, and it is usually important to stay on the path. In some places paths run close to high precipices that might alarm sufferers of vertigo; strong gusts of wind can make walking along narrow paths hazardous, while mists can descend and rapidly reduce visibility in the higher areas. However, provided these factors are borne in mind and proper precautions taken, an averagely fit and steady person can cover all the walks described in this book. Trainers are usually adequate footwear, although walking boots may be preferable. A rope can be helpful on some walks; on some of the steeper coastal paths a stick can be useful – one can often be fashioned along the way. Protection against the sun should be taken on the coastal walks, particularly in the summer. Jumpers might be needed for an early-morning start but usually end up being carried – an anorak is perhaps more practical. Remember to take plenty to drink, especially for the long haul back up from the coast.

The walk descriptions include notes on picnic sites and suggest convenient places to leave cars. Camping is possible at the end of many of the coastal paths, and a swim can be an additional attraction on some walks. Although sharks are present offshore, there is no record of anyone being attacked while bathing off St Helena's rocks (in his book on St Helena's fish, A. Edwards maintains that sharks stay in the main fishing grounds and do not venture inshore). Potential swimmers are more likely to encounter problems from the strong and changeable swell, which can make exiting from the sea hazardous at very short notice.

St Helena's climate can be a deterrent to walking, particularly in the winter, when the Peaks are probably best avoided. But a determination to set out even on the most depressing morning is frequently rewarded with sunshine by the afternoon – particularly on coastal walks, which involve walking to the edges of the island where the cloud cover is lightest. Like the flora, fauna and topography, the weather varies considerably over small distances; a walk might start in wet and cloudy conditions on Deadwood Plain and end in bright sunshine at Banks Battery.

The combination of routes is endless, and someone living on the island will be able to explore fishermen's paths that the casual visitor will never see. Anyone visiting with perhaps only a week to spare should certainly attempt the obvious walks to Mundens and Banks Battery. Apart from these, probably *the* walk to go on is Walk 12 – the one to Lot's Wife Ponds.

'Landing from the mail steamer: heavy rollers on.' (Graphic 1877)

A Walk around Jamestown

The walk starts from the lower steps of the Wharf where all passengers land today – and where Governor Massingham delighted the Press when he missed his footing and received a soaking while assisting Prince Andrew ashore in 1984. You will notice that ships anchor well out in the roadstead. There, in over 17 fathoms, they are safe from the effect of the local rollers which wrecked the Wharf in 1846. The Wharf was entirely rebuilt and subsequently reconstructed in 1914.

There are several wrecks in James Bay – including some Portuguese and Dutch East Indiamen of the early 17th century, but the only visible evidence of disaster is the steering gear of the SS *Papanui*, which sank on fire in 1911. Occasionally from the cliffs above Jamestown an oil slick can still be seen marking the grave of HMS *Darkdale*, an oil carrier torpedoed in 1941.

Walking along the Wharf you pass the various customs sheds and offices. A recent construction of wire, timber and iron cladding replaced a previous building destroyed by a major rockfall. The small red building with a round roof is the old mortuary, dating from 1787. Passing through the passengers' exit gate, the road continues along the fortifications which form part of the Jamestown lines. A number of 32-pounder cannons stand outside the Jubilee Coldstore; they were last fired at the time of the removal of Napoleon's remains in 1840.

Entry into Grand Parade is via a recent archway (reconstructed in 1989) which supports the coat of arms of the East India Company; the coat of arms was made in 1832, the year that the East India Company handed over control of St Helena to the Crown. The old entrance lies through another archway which now leads to the swimming pool changing rooms. The Grand Parade is a relic of the days when the island housed a large military garrison. Immediately on the left is the Castle, which for 300 years has been the offices of the Government of St Helena. The building has been greatly modified and developed in the intervening years and was used as the Governor's Residence until the mid-19th century. Its military function ceased at an early date with the construction of the fort on Ladder Hill.

Just outside the Castle lies a 'post stone' used by the *Dolphin*, and probably many other ships, as a place to leave mail in the 16th and early 17th centuries, before the island was settled by the English. In the middle of Grand Parade stands a monument to Dr Arnold, former surgeon, acting governor and 'the greatest friend St Helena ever had'. Opposite the Castle stands the East India Company's old customs bonded warehouse. To the left a narrow street leads to the foot of the Ladder (Walk 2). The prison, with room for only three inmates, lies next to St James' Church, and dates from the early 19th century.

A Christian place of worship has stood on or close to the present site of St James' Church since about 1540. This has a claim to being one of the earliest Christian sites south of the Equator. The present church was built in 1765. A spire was added later, but unfortunately this distinctive feature of Jamestown became unsafe and was removed in 1982. Inside, the church contains a number of interesting monuments, and outside are now kept many of the memorial stones removed from the town's disused cemeteries.

Opposite St James' lies the police station, the court house and the library. All these buildings were constructed under the orders of Sir Hudson Lowe in 1817.

Main Street stretches from the church to the post office and until about 1860 was the principal residential area. Immediately above the Public Gardens (Walk 2) is the site of the house where Napoleon spent his first night on the island and was much

Upper part of Main Street, Jamestown. (G. W. Melliss)

'Types to be met with on the Streets of Jamestown.' (*Graphic* 1877)

inconvenienced by the crowds gazing at him. The present building used to be the Paramount Cinema but is now a garage. The next building is Broadway House, the ground floor of which houses the museum, open on Saturday mornings and at other times by request: upstairs is the Government Information Office. The blue building on the opposite side of the street is Wellington House Hotel; the building's history is obscure but it is unlikely that Wellington ever stayed here (Walk 16).

There are several other distinguished buildings on both sides of Main Street. At the top of the street are the post office, originally constructed as an officer's mess and later used to house the lace school until 1917, and opposite, the Consulate Hotel with its intricate wrought iron balcony and verandah; around the turn of the century it was known as the Royal Hotel, but its present name is in memory of its use as the American Consulate from 1847.

At the head of Main Street is the impressive Victorian Malabar Store, now Solomons warehouse and the Canister, rebuilt by PWSD in the 1950s. It houses the handicraft shop. Outside are two peepul trees, an avenue of which used to line Main Street. The trees provide a nice reminder of St Helena's long association with India, for it was under the peepul or sacred bo tree that the Buddha attained Nirvana. In contrast, in Jamestown 'under the trees' signified the site for the slave market before emancipation in 1832.

From the Canister follow Napoleon Street until a narrow fork leads off to the right. This back lane leads down to the Government Garage and then across the Run (Walk 2) to Seale's Corner on Market Street. Here a left turn will take you towards the hospital and the road up Ladder Hill, while a right turn will take you back to Main Street. Just before rejoining Main Street, you pass the Victorian wrought iron public market building which was refurbished and reopened during 1990.

'Jamestown from the Side Path looking north.' (Graphic 1890)

Coastal Walks

'View of Island from the Sea.' (Graphic 1877)

1 Breakneck Valley

Elevation range: 200m – sea level
Length: 1km each way

The walk to Breakneck Valley is short and offers a good afternoon excursion for a swim. In the early days sailors used to report that you were liable to break your heart going up the hills of St Helena and break your neck going down. Why this description should have been applied to this particular valley is unclear, for the way down is relatively easily negotiated. Nevertheless the penalties of straying off even an easy path are illustrated by the experience of a sailor from the *Wyndham* in 1734. Having been up country until after dark, he attempted to take a short cut back to his ship via the cliffs around Breakneck Valley. He reached a point where he could go neither up nor down and had to await daylight. At last he managed to attract the attention of a boat passing below and in the end he was rescued by rope. The account ends: 'he lost a china bowl and a catty of tea which none of our people, not even the blacks, have ventured to go there and fetch'.

A car can be left on the main road by Verandah Quarters or driven some way down the track to where, at the time of writing, waste stabilization ponds are being constructed to take the sewage from Half Tree Hollow. Below this the rifle range stretches down to the edge of the cliff. The start of the path down the side of Breakneck Valley is not obvious but can be found by first following the concrete path down the rifle range and then cutting across to the left edge of the valley where a rusty iron pole marks the top of the downward route.

The descent takes about a quarter of an hour. As with many other small valleys, Breakneck was walled up as part of the 18th-century defence system. Although the wall is still largely preserved, the climb down is easy.

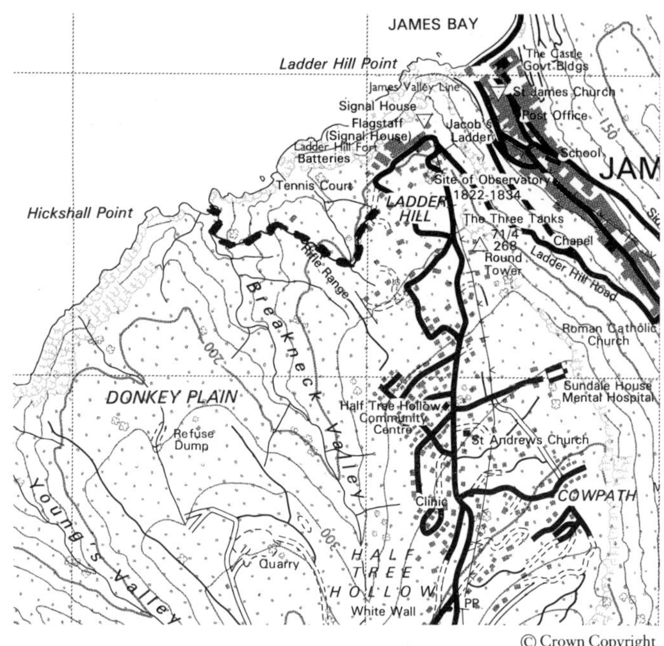

Along the bottom of the valley prickly pear, or tungi, are common. This plant has generally been considered undesirable and partly successful attempts were made to eradicate it by introducing a grub that completely destroys the plant, leaving just a grey skeleton. Tungi fruit can be eaten but caution is required when picking and peeling to avoid the small hairs which are a major skin irritant; the effort is scarcely worthwhile, although the fruit is said to make good wine. Another plant common in Breakneck, and many other valleys, is St Helena samphire; this is a low woody shrub with grey-green leaves that has an unpleasant smell.

There was considerable excitement in 1708 when a councillor, Captain Mashbone, reported the discovery of gold and silver ore in Breakneck Valley; this sparked a gold rush which was encouraged by the Governor at the time, Captain Roberts. But, as Gosse reports, 'Alas for false hopes, Captain Mashbone's gold proved, on being assayed in England, to be nothing but iron pyrites'.

Swimming from the rocks usually presents no difficulties, and an area of submerged rocks on the point makes for some good snorkelling. However, care is required when a large swell is running. Some way offshore there is an artificial reef which is the dumping site for St Helena's wrecked cars. The reef is an attempt to encourage fish and marine growth.

The cliffs between Breakneck Valley and Jamestown hold a small colony of red-billed tropic birds (known locally as 'trophy birds'), possibly St Helena's most spectacular seabird. The size of a large gull, the tropic bird is predominantly white with fine black barring on the upper parts and has a dagger-like scarlet bill. The central tail feathers are elongated into streamers as long as the body, making adult birds quite unmistakable. Some birds are present around Breakneck Valley throughout the day, but they are most often seen in late afternoon when many return from fishing.

The climb back up the cliff can be accomplished in about half an hour. Very strong swimmers might contemplate swimming back to Jamestown, so long as there is someone to meet them when they arrive at the steps.

2 Mundens – Sampsons Battery – Jamestown

Elevation range: 30 – 270m
Length: 3.5km

This walk starts and finishes in Jamestown. It is a good evening walk – particularly for anyone staying in Jamestown without transport. The start is along Sisters' Walk – so named after the daughters of Governor Patton (1802-07) who had the promenade constructed for their use. It can be reached either via the steps by the side of the Jubilee Coldstore on the Wharf or by walking through the Public Gardens. The gardens were constructed in 1792 by soldiers labouring in lieu of receiving corporal punishment. The building in the rear corner of the gardens (now a private house) was used for a lecture given by Joshua Slocum on 14 April 1898, when he called at St Helena during the first solo circumnavigation of the world in his yacht *Spray*. The content of this lecture is described in Jackson's *St Helena*. In addition, the *Waterwitch* monument in the Public Gardens recalls St Helena's role in the fight against the slave trade. The *Waterwitch* was a sloop that was lost while pursuing slaving ships.

Sisters' Walk joins the old road to Mundens Battery (named after Sir Richard Munden, see Walk 7). Half-way along, a zigzag path leads off up the cliff to Upper Mundens. This is a short cut that misses out Lower Mundens. Lower Mundens Battery was first built immediately after the British recaptured the island from the Dutch in 1673 and was sporadically developed up until the second World War. The searchlight batteries immediately above the end of the Wharf date from this time. The derelict house which forms part of the fortifications was used to house St Helena's most recent political prisoners – three Bahreini princes held from 1957 to 1961.

The path to the upper battery is visible from Lower Mundens. It

'Ladder Hill.' (Graphic 1890)

is also an easy walk to continue on round to Ruperts from here (see Walk 3); on the way it is worth pausing at the promontory known as Chubbs Rock. From here Edward Chubb fell to his death in 1683. In 1846 huge waves washed one of the Chubbs Battery guns into the sea and a similar event had also occurred in 1737.

Returning to the path up the cliff, there are further gun emplacements at Upper Mundens Battery, where walkers who have taken the short cut zigzag path will emerge. The sad ruin on the ridge was finally abandoned in the 1950s after the second of the last occupant's children had fallen to his death over the nearby cliff.

From Upper Mundens there are good views across James Valley, and of Jacob's Ladder. The Ladder was built as a tramway in 1830, mainly for hauling military stores up Ladder Hill. Its operation was never successful and in 1871 it was reconstructed in its present form with 699 steps. The name Ladder Hill predates the tramway by some 150 years and refers to the original rope ladder used to climb the cliff. In the early days of the colony miscreants were hung in chains at the top of the hill to die a gruesome death in full view of the town. The scars of former, frequently fatal, rockfalls mark the sides of Ladder Hill. The worst recorded fall occurred in April 1890 when nine people were killed; a fountain commemorating their deaths used to stand outside the Consulate Hotel.

From September to March St Helena is visited by skuas, large dark-brown gull-like birds, which have migrated from their Arctic breeding grounds to avoid the northern winter. Mundens Battery provides an excellent vantage point from which to watch these pirates robbing returning fairy terns (see Walk 21) of their catch. Skuas patrol James Bay singly or in small groups, well offshore, but flocks may gather at dusk to roost on the sea.

There is no clearly defined path along the top of Ruperts Ridge; the walk continues upwards through the prickly pear as the crest of

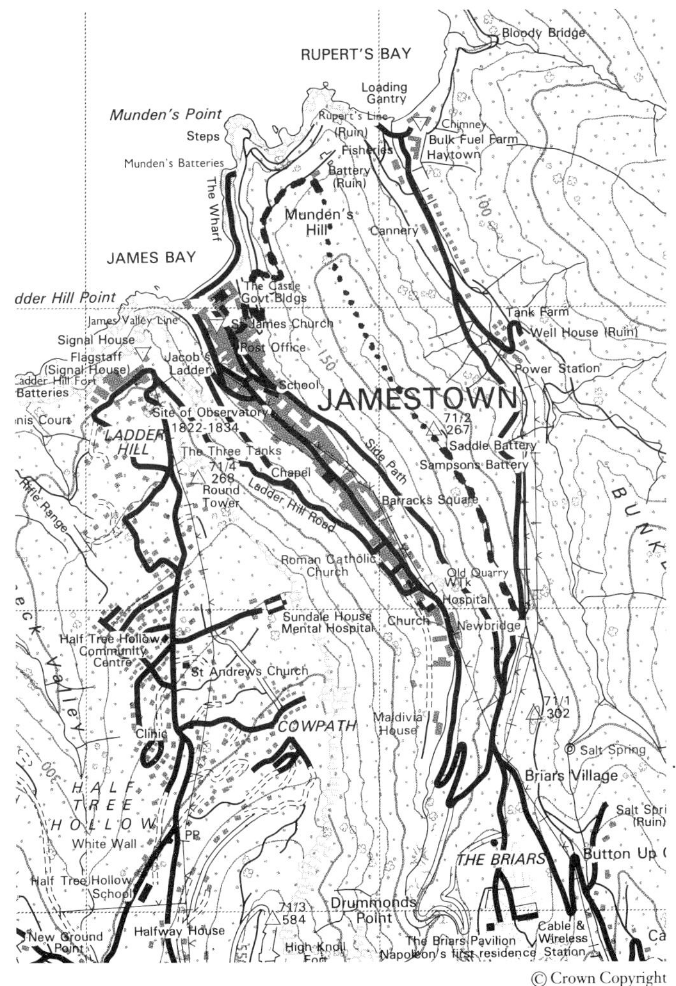

the ridge narrows into a rocky knife edge. For a few paces there is a dizzy drop to Jamestown on one side and Ruperts on the other; after this point the ridge widens again and is occupied by Saddle and Sampsons Batteries. The latter has some of the best preserved cannon on St Helena.

From the batteries it is a short walk down to Field Road, which connects Jamestown to Ruperts (named after Governor Sir John Field, 1962-68). From here you can descend to Ruperts and return to Jamestown by the coast path (Walk 3), but a walk down Sidepath is more rewarding (and quicker). There are fine views of upper Jamestown. Of particular note is the view of the Run, as the James Valley stream is known. It is largely walled in and invisible from adjacent streets; a walk along it from the Hospital to just above the back of Musk's store provides an attractive back view of Jamestown. You can see the spring line on the side of High Knoll causing a patch of straight-edged vegetation on the barren hillside. The spring is caused by the impermeable red tuff (volcanic ash) which has been overlain by more permeable lavas through which water can move more easily; this formation is common on the island. There is also a good view of the old Cowpath winding up the cliff to Half Tree Hollow. It was constructed to enable cattle grazing on the pastures, now occupied by Maldivia, to be moved quickly inland at times of threat from strange ships.

3 Deadwood – Pipe Path – Ruperts

Elevation range: 525m – sea level
Length: 3km

This walk is best accomplished by starting at Deadwood and proceeding down to pre-arranged transport at Ruperts, although a circuit is possible for the fit and enthusiastic.

The Pipe Path takes its name from the route taken by a pipe that was laid to take water from a desalinization plant at Ruperts to the Boer prisoners on Deadwood Plain. The restored chimney within the Bulk Fuel Farm in Ruperts marks the site of the plant but, apart from a brief trial, the plant was never used.

The walk starts in the north-western corner of Deadwood pastures. Initially the route follows the track along the crest of Banks Ridge. The views across to High Knoll, Francis Plain and beyond are excellent if the weather is fine. Efforts have been made to halt the erosion on the ridge by digging soil conservation ditches and replanting with hardy shrubs, trees and aloes. The track continues to the triangulation point at the end of the ridge from where you can see the path down to Ruperts; the descent is straightforward, although care needs to be taken to avoid the prickly pear.

The origin of the name of the bay is somewhat obscure. According to an entry in the St Helena Records, Prince Rupert, the famous cavalry leader of the English Civil War, anchored in the bay on his return from India. It is also said that he hid in the bay in 1651 in order to attack the Dutch or British Indiamen *en route* to Europe. Neither story can be verified, although Prince Rupert visited both Cape Verde and the Gambia in 1652.

The path emerges by the old chimney. The remains of Ruperts Valley fortifications run along the other side of the Fuel Farm. Ruperts fortified line is one of the longest on the island and was improved and developed throughout the 18th century. Flanking protection was added on Mundens Hill, and at Saddle and Sampsons Batteries (Walk 2). Unfortunately Ruperts Line is disintegrating rapidly; however, the new sea wall will afford better protection from the waves.

There are a number of alternatives to taking a vehicle to Ruperts. One option is to take the coast walk back to Jamestown, joining up with Walk 2 at Mundens – the path can be seen leading up the west side of Ruperts Valley. An old sign warns of the dangers of this route (because a rockfall has undercut the path at one point), but the path is often used. Another alternative is to walk up the floor of Ruperts Valley and to take the Boer Path back up to Deadwood.

The west slope of Ruperts has been planted with 'aloes' that are strictly agaves. The plant is common in dry areas and has a number of species, all of which send up flowering poles. There have been various unsuccessful attempts to use the plant commercially. By the road is a small avenue of coconuts planted in the 1980s; so far they have survived, but historically coconuts have not been successful on St Helena because the rainfall is too low. After the coconuts the route passes the site of the old liberated slave quarters. The Royal Navy used St Helena as a base from which to suppress the West African slave trade by intercepting the slavers and releasing their cargoes on St Helena (see the *Waterwitch* monument, Walk 2). Just over 9,000 slaves were received at St Helena between 1840 and 1847. Of these about 3,000 died during the liberating process and the majority of the remainder emigrated, leaving some 450 new settlers on the island. Most of the old quarters are now covered by the new power station built in 1985.

As you continue up the valley, vegetation increases and water appears in the stream, although it is very saline. The start of the path back up to Deadwood is marked by a solitary palm tree. The

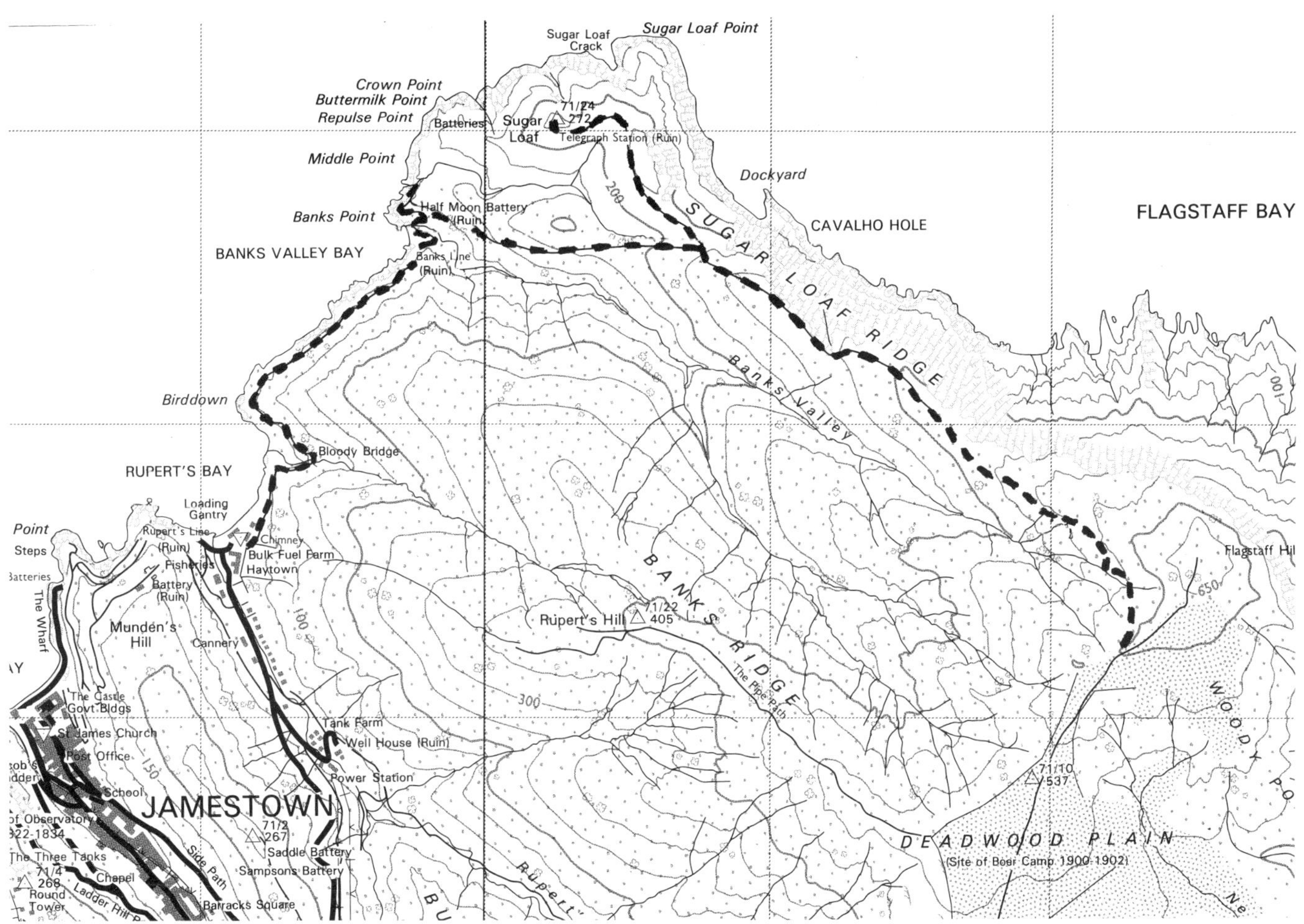

Sugar Loaf Point
Sugar Loaf Crack
Crown Point
Buttermilk Point
Repulse Point
Batteries
Sugar Loaf
71/24
272
Telegraph Station (Ruin)
Middle Point
Dockyard
Banks Point
Half Moon Battery (Ruin)
SUGAR LOAF RIDGE
CAVALHO HOLE
FLAGSTAFF BAY
BANKS VALLEY BAY
Banks Line (Ruin)
Banks Valley
Birddown
Bloody Bridge
RUPERT'S BAY
Loading Gantry
Point
Steps
Batteries
Rupert's Line (Ruin)
Chimney
Bulk Fuel Farm
Haytown
Fisheries
Battery (Ruin)
The Wharf
Munden's Hill
Cannery
BANKS RIDGE
Rupert's Hill
71/22
405
Flagstaff Hil
650
The Castle
Govt Bldgs
St James Church
Post Office
Tank Farm
Well House (Ruin)
The Pipe Path
WOODY
Power Station
School
JAMESTOWN
Observatory
71/2
267
71/10
537
The Three Tanks
71/4
268
Round Tower
Chapel
Ladder Hill
Saddle Battery
Sampsons Battery
Side Path
Barracks Square
DEADWOOD PLAIN
(Site of Boer Camp 1900-1902)

'The "first" photograph of the wirebird.' (Illustrated London News 1956)

path was constructed, or at least upgraded, by the Boers. The walk up the valley side is not easy as the path is not always clear, and the prickly pear stands ready to punish any momentary lapse in concentration.

4 Flagstaff Hill – Banks Battery – Ruperts

Elevation range: 600m – sea level
Length: 6km (including Sugar Loaf)

This is a one-way walk that starts at Deadwood and finishes at Ruperts. The start is not readily obvious but takes off through a gap in the fence on the left of the route up Flagstaff (see Walk 5). In wet weather the first stretch, across the eroded country immediately below Flagstaff, is muddy and slippery but once you reach Sugar Loaf Ridge the walk becomes an easy downhill stroll with spectacular views and drops on the seaward side. On the landward side you can see the recent successful efforts to reafforest the head of Banks Valley. The endemic scrubwood grows fairly extensively along the ridge and is identified by its low bush shape and daisy-like flowers.

Along the route there is a fishermen's path leading to Cavalho Hole and the Dockyard. 'Path' is euphemistic, since it comprises a length of cable leading down an extremely steep gully. The hole is named after the cavalley fish, which is a type of jack often found near steep rock faces.

After 2 - 2.5km the path splits and the more energetic walker can take a diversion to the right up Sugar Loaf before continuing down to Banks Battery. Sugar Loaf is climbed by the remains of what was once a high quality track used for manning the signal station on the summit. Unfortunately the last part of the path has slipped away so that reaching the top involves a scramble. The view from the top is magnificent. Its former importance as a signalling station is apparent when it is remembered that in a large sailing ship the only way to approach Jamestown was to hug the leeward shore after rounding Sugar Loaf Point, and to use the ship's way to reach the Roads. In 1877 there was an altercation when the old flagstaff on Sugar Loaf 'was hewn down and burnt by Yon, by direction of the

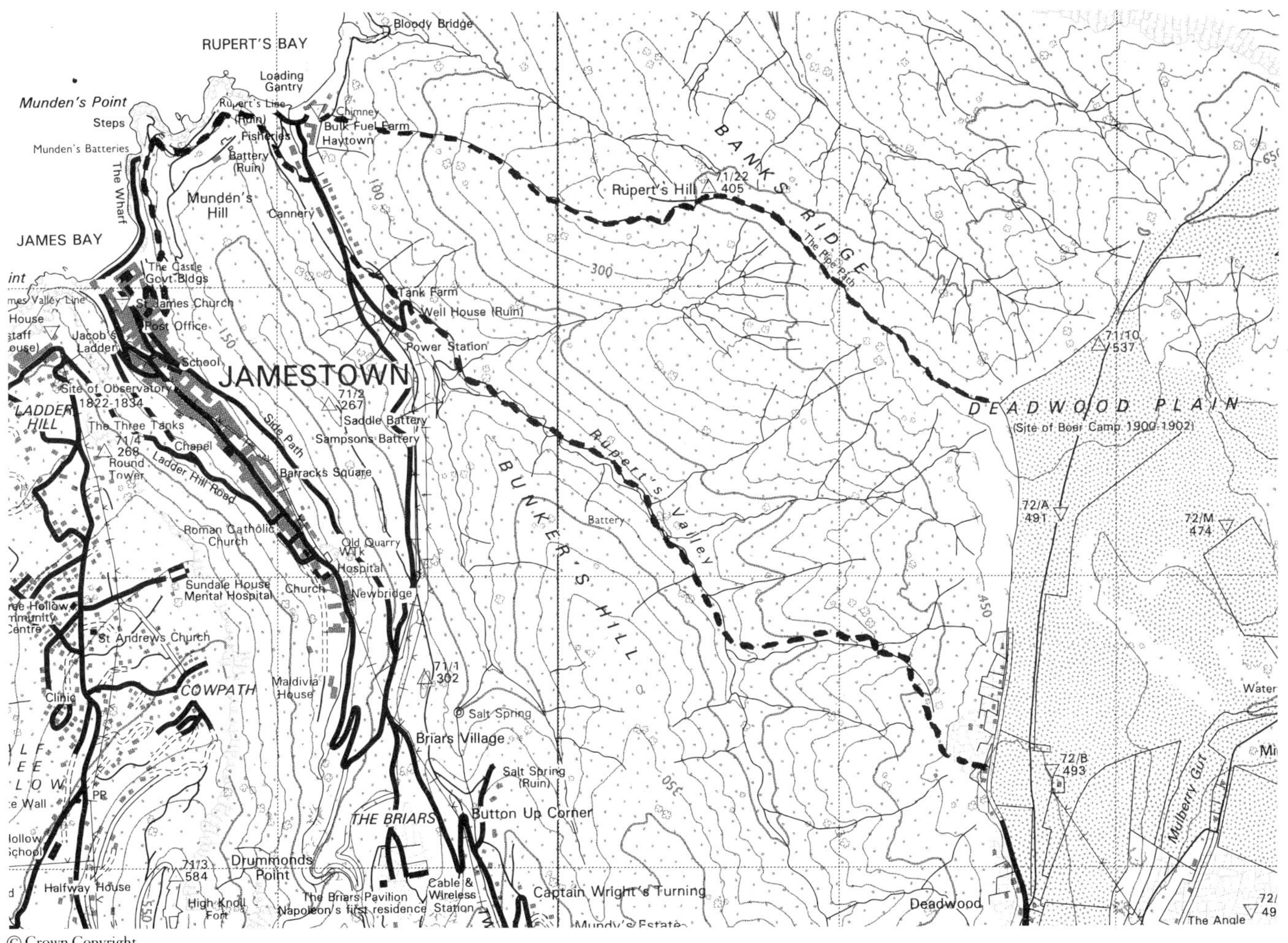
RUPERT'S BAY
Bloody Bridge
Loading Gantry
Munden's Point
Steps
Munden's Batteries
Rupert's Line (Ruin)
Chimney
Bulk Fuel Farm
Haytown
Fisheries
Battery (Ruin)
The Wharf
Munden's Hill
Cannery
JAMES BAY
The Castle
Govt Bldgs
St James Church
Post Office
Jacob's Ladder
School
JAMESTOWN
Tank Farm
Well House (Ruin)
Power Station
Site of Observatory 1822-1834
LADDER HILL
The Three Tanks
71/4 268
Round Tower
Chapel
Ladder Hill Road
Side Path
71/2 267
Saddle Battery
Sampsons Battery
Barracks Square
Roman Catholic Church
Old Quarry
WTk
Hospital
Sundale House Mental Hospital
Church
Newbridge
St Andrews Church
COWPATH
Clinic
Maldivia House
71/1 302
Salt Spring
Briars Village
Salt Spring (Ruin)
Button Up Corner
THE BRIARS
71/3 584
Drummonds Point
Halfway House
High Knoll Fort
The Briars Pavilion
Napoleon's first residence
Cable & Wireless Station
Captain Wright's Turning
Mundy's Estate
BANKS RIDGE
The Pipe Path
Rupert's Hill
71/22 405
Rupert's Valley
BUNKER'S HILL
Battery
DEADWOOD PLAIN
(Site of Boer Camp 1900-1902)
71/10 537
72/A 491
72/M 474
72/B 493
Mulberry Gut
Deadwood
The Angle
Water
100
150
300
350
450
550
650

colonial engineer', for it had been an important landmark from the sea for nearly two hundred years.

Sugar Loaf is part of the original volcano that was centred around the north-east corner of the island. Activity in this area ceased about 11 million years ago, but the laval flows are visible, particularly on the section of the walk between Banks and Ruperts.

From the point where the paths split, some care is needed on the final descent to Banks Battery. Originally the path was a high quality mule track connecting the lower batteries with the signal station. However, it is now badly eroded, and there are prickly pears obstructing parts of the track.

The network of fortifications loosely referred to as Banks Battery are among the most interesting on the island. Because of the method of approaching the Roads in a sailing ship they were of strategic importance. The spot was fortified as early as 1678 and the fortifications continued to be improved for the next 150 years. The original fortification consisted of 'Bankses Platform' (named after the officer in charge of its construction) behind the walled up valley but this was washed away and rebuilt in Napoleonic times. The new fort was guarded by the cannon that are still lying on the platform. A tunnel was built under the wall to carry storm water and the slots of a portcullis are visible. Later the main battery, first known as King William's Fort and then as Half Moon Battery, was built and is well preserved; its guns lie in the water beneath the battery. In 1778 the East India Company decided to extend the fortifications around the cliff from Half Moon and three further batteries named Repulse Point, Middle Point and Buttermilk Point were constructed. These can be reached by the track from Half Moon. In 1787 a board was provided at Buttermilk Point instructing, in large letters, all ships to 'send a boat' to establish credentials. The Heritage Society had recently embarked upon a campaign to preserve the batteries.

Swimming in Banks Bay is pleasant and relatively safe most of the time but, as elsewhere, caution is needed because of the unexpectedly quick change in the swell. The walk back to Ruperts is by way of the coast path that leads off from the west side of Banks Valley. The path was restored in 1989 so that it now offers a good walk. Towards the end of the path there is a good view of the Bulk Fuel Farm, which is particularly dramatic when a ship is discharging its load.

The route from either Ruperts or Jamestown to Banks and return is a variation of this walk that makes a pleasant and easy-going afternoon outing.

The summit of Sugar Loaf. (Burchell)

5 Flagstaff Hill – Knotty Ridge – The Barn

Elevation range: 400 – 600m
Length: 3km each way

Approach Flagstaff across Deadwood Plain. In dry weather you can drive across the Plain and up the lower slopes of the hill. However, the walk across Deadwood is worthwhile quite apart from fine views and open pasture land.

The early ravages of goat and man soon destroyed the original vegetation (mainly gumwoods), but by doing this they probably improved the habitat for the wirebird. The wirebird is a small, long-legged, grey-brown plover with white underparts and a black mask extending to the sides of the neck. It is found only on St Helena. With a current population of around 500 individuals it is one of the rarest birds in the world. Wirebirds mainly inhabit the drier grasslands and semi-desert areas of the island where they feed on beetles. Their nest is a simple scrape in the earth in which two mottled eggs are laid, mainly between October and March. The chicks leave the nest within 24 hours of hatching. Both eggs and chicks are very well camouflaged, but if you accidentally disturb a nest let the parent return as soon as possible and do not touch the eggs. Wirebirds are thought to be descended from a flock of plovers blown off course from Africa several thousand years ago.

A concrete strip marks one of the sites of an army cricket pitch installed in the 1950s (there is another at Blue Hill, which is still used occasionally). From about 1816 until at least 1875, Deadwood was used as a racecourse as well as a military encampment. It was also the site of one of the Boer prisoner of war camps from 1900 to 1902 (see also Walk 19).

Flagstaff, despite its name, was not successful as a signalling station because of the frequency of summit mists, and the station was moved to Prosperous Bay as early as 1692 (although it was briefly resurrected during Napoleon's captivity). The route to the top of the hill is easy, but once at the summit after a relatively gentle climb, it is a shock to be confronted by cliffs dropping away 600m to the sea.

The path to the Barn can be reached by a scramble down the south-east side of Flagstaff or by cutting eastwards across the last pasture before the top of Flagstaff. At the eastern edge of the pasture climb under the barbed wire fence, and the path to Knotty Ridge leads across eroded country which supports a solitary windswept tree.

Connecting Knotty Ridge and the Barn is a knife-edge ridge with sharp drops on either side; the path runs on the contour, just below the ridge crest. In fact the most difficult part of the walk is the descent from Knotty Ridge down a steep, slippery slope on to the knife-edge ridge. Considerable care is needed here. Thereafter you can relax and admire the massive dyke swarms (injections of igneous rock that cut across the formation of older rocks) of Knotty Ridge that so fascinated Charles Darwin in 1836 when he visited St Helena in the *Beagle*, towards the end of his four-year voyage. The route on to the Barn is relatively straightforward with a stepped climb up a low cliff which leads on to the lower slopes. The summit is covered by mesembryanthemum and is flat apart from the little pinnacle known as the Haystack. There are superb views across to Longwood.

The Barn is arguably St Helena's most famous landmark. When approaching from Ascension it is, with Flagstaff, the first land to appear over the horizon. It comprises the oldest rocks on the island, some of which, notably on Knotty Ridge, were formed before St Helena emerged from the sea. On these rocks were laid the hard resistant lavas that form the Barn. The Barn was said to have depressed Napoleon during his captivity at Longwood and he described it as 'The Grim Old Sentinel'. When his body was exhumed in 1840, to be taken back to France, a romantically

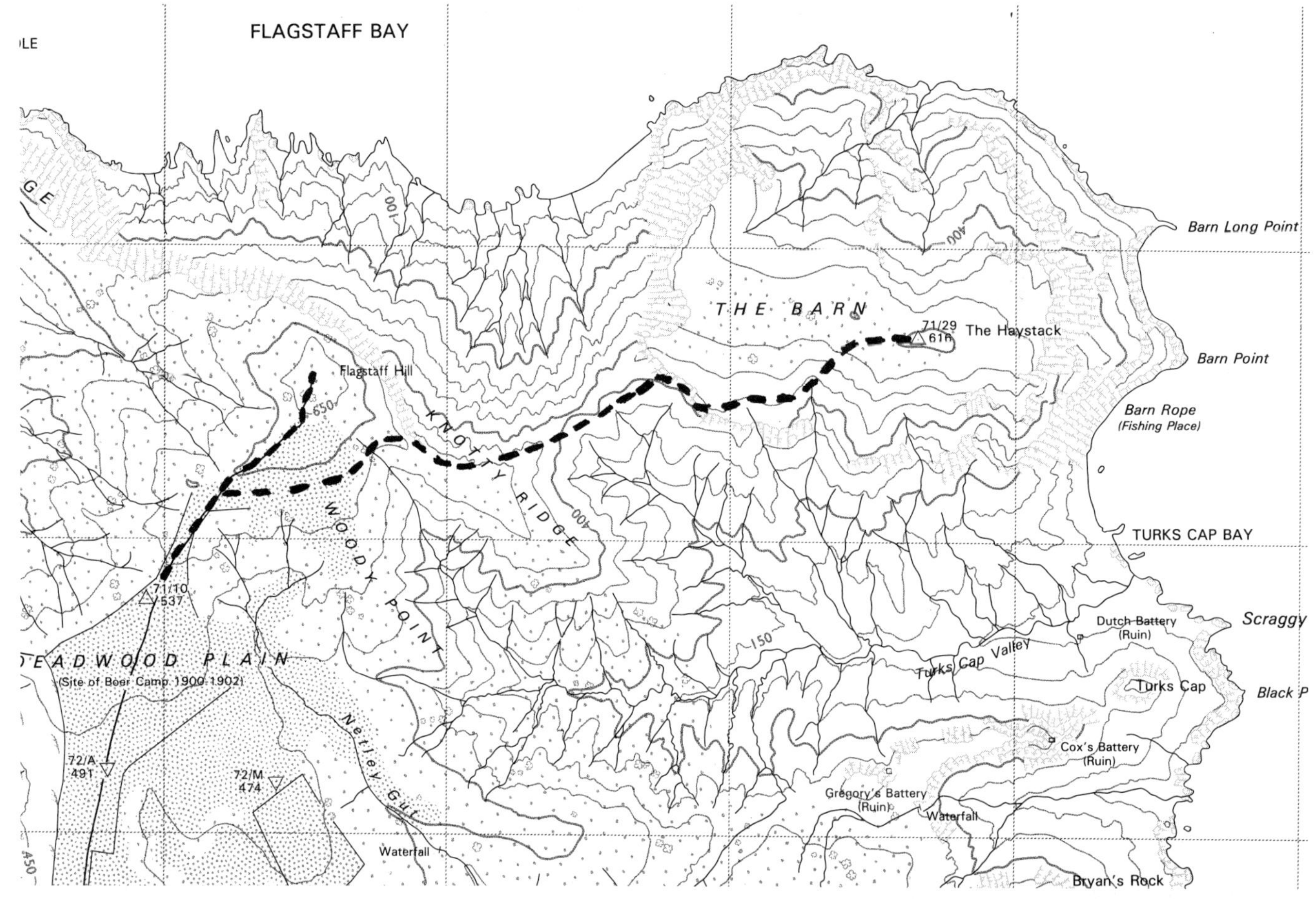
FLAGSTAFF BAY
THE BARN
71/29
61ft
The Haystack
Barn Long Point
Barn Point
Barn Rope
(Fishing Place)
Flagstaff Hill
650
KNOTTY RIDGE
WOODY POINT
TURKS CAP BAY
71/10
537
Dutch Battery
(Ruin)
Scraggy
Turks Cap Valley
Turks Cap
Black P
DEADWOOD PLAIN
(Site of Boer Camp 1900-1902)
Netley Gut
72/A
491
72/M
474
Cox's Battery
(Ruin)
Gregory's Battery
(Ruin)
Waterfall
Bryan's Rock
150
400
100
450

inclined Frenchman thought that its shape resembled that of the former Emperor's death mask.

The Barn was also one of the last outposts of wild goats until quite recently. At the end of the 18th century a hermit, known as London's Ben, would go missing on the Barn for long periods when the 'White Goat' called. In 1807, over 20 years after his final disappearance, some men shooting goats found a path leading to some small caves in the side of a precipice containing the remains of habitation – thought to be Ben's hideaway.

The outward walk is completed by climbing the rocky knoll called the Haystack on the Barn's summit. The way home is via the same route but the return to Knotty Ridge, being up rather than down, is easier than on the way out.

*The term gut, meaning stream, is used on a number of former British colonial islands. On St Helena guts discharge into valleys but not direct into the sea although Broad Gut is the most obvious exception to this rule.

6 Turks Cap Valley

Elevation range: 475m – sea level – 435m
Length: 7.5km round trip

This walk starts by taking the road that follows the west side of Longwood Farm, after parking at the end of the tarmac. Since the end of the walk is at the Bottom Woods Weather Station, it is advisable to leave a second car there to avoid a long walk back across Bottom Woods Paddocks and Longwood Farm. The path starts by following round the lower slopes of Middle Point before dropping down on to the floor of Mulberry Gut.* There is no clearly defined path down the gut, but it is a pleasant walk across pastures and around the sides of two waterfalls. On the right-hand side are the remains of a long stone wall. This was the wall built in the 1720s in order to try to protect the young gumwoods of the Great Wood from the ravages of goats. Unfortunately neither the wall nor the protection policy was maintained and the woodland was lost (hence the name Deadwood).

Some way farther on you reach the junction with Netley Gut and there are fine views back up the valley towards Flagstaff. Bilberry Gut then joins the main gut from the other (south) side. At this level much of the vegetation cover has gone and the walk continues over highly eroded country that provides easy walking when dry but extremely slippery conditions when wet (Walk 8). The valley bottom remains green but becomes wider and also increasingly boggy. After a few hundred metres the hill on the left side of the valley becomes lower and finally disappears to reveal Turks Cap Valley falling away below but running parallel to Mulberry Gut. This rather odd feature provides a text-book example of stream capture. Mulberry Gut used to flow due east, over a high waterfall and enter the sea to the south of Turks Cap. In times of flood it still does this, but for the rest of time the flow

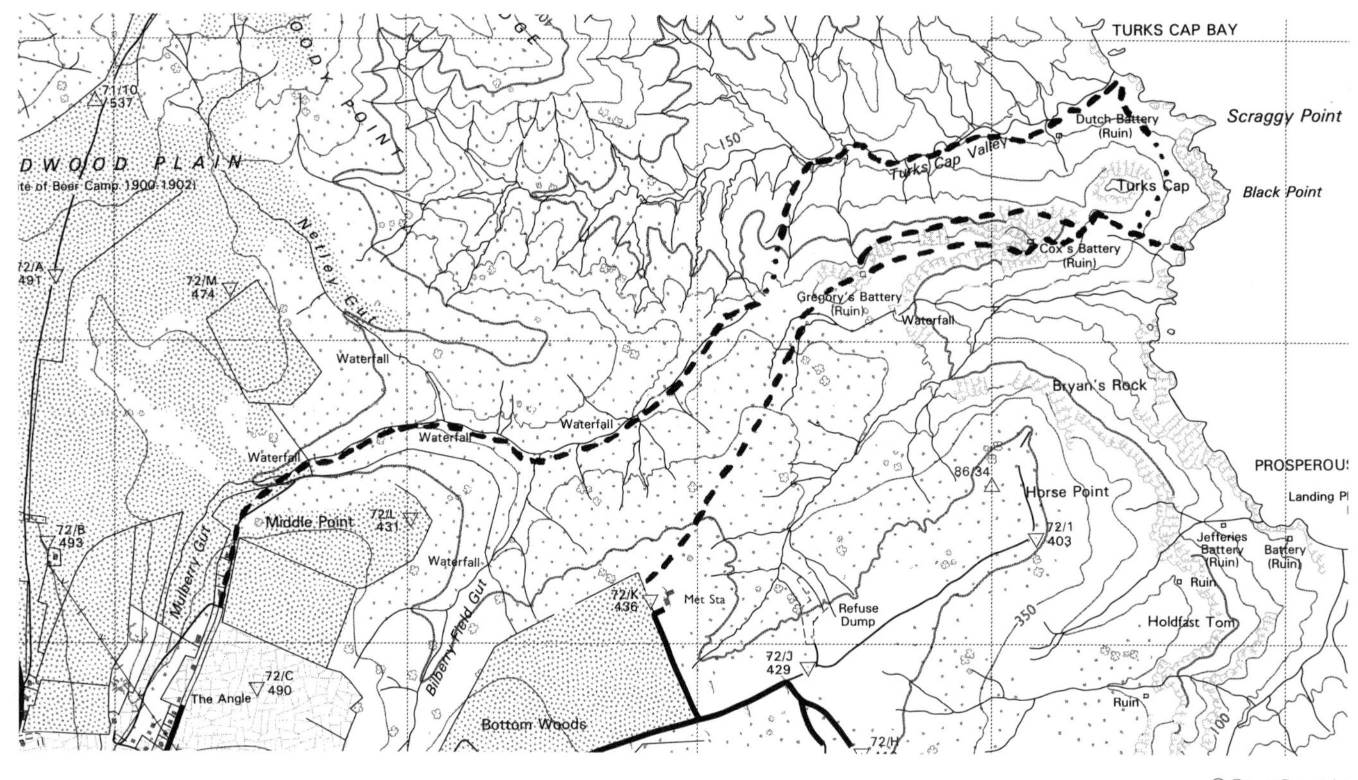

© Crown Copyright

takes a sharp right angle north and drops into Turks Cap Valley. The soft side slopes of Turks Cap Valley have been eroded back to allow the capture to occur.

At this point there are various options. A turn to the right up the mesembryanthemum-covered slope will take you back to the weather station; the path is seen easily from the opposite hillside, but not so easily from the valley floor. One alternative is to take the path to Gregory's and Cox's Batteries, but probably the most interesting is to scramble down one of the scree-covered slopes to the floor of Turks Cap Valley. The slope indicated on the map does not present a serious obstacle. On the way down you can see the old Cornelian mine on the opposite side of the valley.

Originally excavated on the orders of Governor Beatson in the early 19th century and later developed by the Boers, it is little more than a hole in the ground which has largely been refilled. Cornelian is a red form of silica known as chalcedony and is semi-precious. It is formed by the heat of intruded dykes passing through lava flows. Some relatively large stones are owned by islanders and the mine is surrounded by small fragments.

From the mine it is possible to reach the sea by following the stream down Turks Cap Valley. The stream cuts through the end of the Knotty Ridge dyke swarms (Walk 5) which have been exposed by erosion. The remains of an old battery dominate the outlet of the valley to the sea. Variously known as Portugee or Dutch Battery, the remains are in fact contemporaneous with the island's other coastal defences, being constructed in 1734.

From the sea there are alternative routes back. One path leads around the seaward side of Turks Cap; it soon peters out, but a relatively safe traverse can be made over the boulder slopes of Turks Cap before joining up with the well-defined path that leads from Cox's Battery to Black Point. Alternatively it is possible to traverse around the landward side of Turks Cap, but the paths in this area are generally not very good. Having reached the cliff below Cox's Battery it is possible either to climb to the battery (with difficulty) and proceed along the ridge back to the point of stream capture, or to proceed along the northern side of the cliff under Cox's Battery, eventually emerging at Gregory's Battery; this route offers a better defined path. A soldier is said to have committed suicide at Gregory's by throwing himself over the precipice and his supposed hand print can still be seen.

Having returned to the point of stream capture take the path back up to the Bottom Woods Weather Station. Balloons for observing the upper atmosphere are released from the station every morning and evening and on clear days can be seen during the course of the walk.

7 Prosperous Bay

Elevation range: 300m – sea level
Length: 2.5km each way

The route to Prosperous Bay follows lower Fisher's Valley. In dry conditions cars can be driven down and parked on Prosperous Bay Plain, but in wet weather it is advisable to walk from the Government workshop at Bradleys. The track crosses Fisher's Valley at Cook's Bridge (named after the Diplomatic Wireless Service rigger who supervised the construction of the bridge in the late 1960s). Although saline, there is almost always water flowing at this point in an otherwise rather bare and eroded area. Two salt-loving plants – mesembryanthemum and old man salt bush – are common; the latter is used as a cattle browse. The spot is a favourite haunt of moorhens and wirebirds (see Walk 25).

The track continues to Prosperous Bay Plain. Pockets of gypsum (an evaporite) suggest that the Plain may have been formed below sea level and raised to its present position. This gypsum, as plaster of Paris, was used to make Napoleon's death mask. In the post-war years the southern end of the Plain supported a network of radio masts run by the Diplomatic Wireless Service for monitoring radio traffic from West Africa. Only a few rusty relics remain (Walk 25). The Plain is the site for the proposed airstrip and the line of the approximately north-south runway is marked by stakes. On the far side of the Plain the old signal station provides an excellent view down to Prosperous Bay (see Other Walks).

The path leaves the Plain just below the first main waterfall on the east side of the valley. The first few metres can be a bit of a shock to inexperienced walkers, particularly when wet, as the path is steep, slippery and above a large drop. Once this has been negotiated, the path is fairly easy. After a few hundred metres it

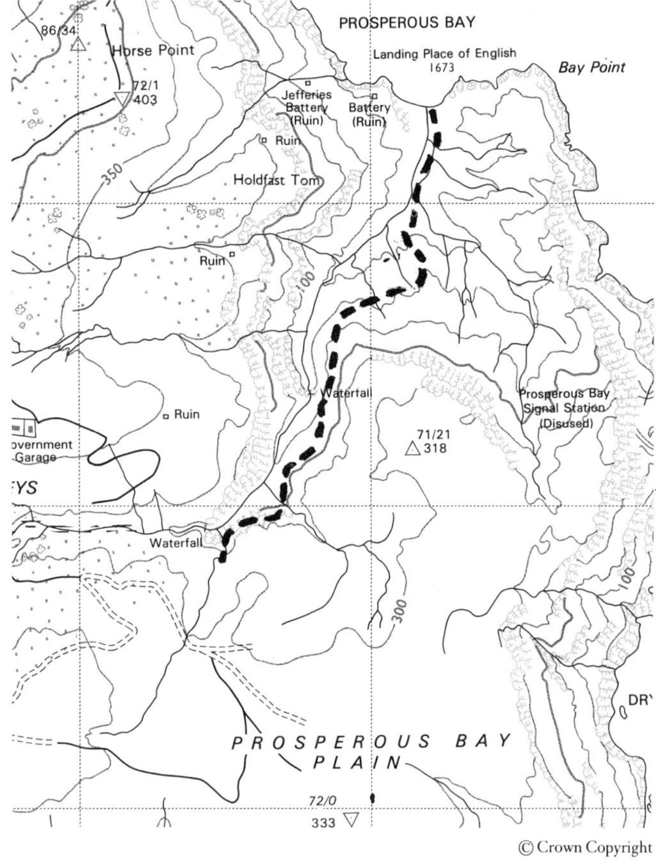

© Crown Copyright

splits for a time into upper and lower levels; there is little difference between the two, although the lower path is less vertiginous.

During wet weather this walk provides good views of the waterfalls that are among the highest and largest flowing on the island. The path gradually drops down the side of the valley; care is needed where there is loose scree but the route is safe for children. Finally the path drops quickly to the valley floor and the last stages of the walk follow the stream. Bones of many birds in the banks of the stream are the remains of seabird colonies that existed up to the time of St Helena's discovery. Bone deposits have also been discovered at Sugar Loaf, Dry Gut, Sandy Bay and Donkey Plain. The seabird colonies were dominated by burrow-nesting petrels and shearwaters, some of which were unique. The colonies fell victim to the introduction of cats and the only seabirds that have survived are those that nest high up on cliffs.

The ghostly white fairy terns with their translucent wings and dark eyes are among the most beautiful of all seabirds and are common on this walk. They are often extremely inquisitive and will hover only a few feet from passers-by, thus providing an excellent opportunity for photographs. Fairy terns are unusual in that they build no nest. This is all the more remarkable in those that lay their eggs in trees, the single egg being precariously balanced in a hollow on a branch. Not surprisingly many eggs and chicks are lost in high winds. The majority of fairy terns, however, nest in the greater safety of cliff ledges and some breed on buildings in Jamestown; St James' Church is a favoured site. The fairy tern has calls consisting of nasal grunts and squeaks, which may continue long after darkness.

St Helena was captured by the Dutch on New Year's Day 1673 but the British retook it on the following 5 May. While a naval bombardment was effected by Sir Richard Munden on Jamestown, Lieutenant Keigwin made a landing with 350 men in Prosperous

Bay on the rocks now known as Keigwin's Point. Having disembarked, the troops were guided up the cliffs by the slave Black Oliver. Although initially easy, the final climb might have been impossible but for a soldier named Tom who managed to pull himself on to a convenient ledge and let a rope down for his comrades. As they swarmed up they shouted 'Holdfast Tom' and the cliff was thus named. (The point is passed on the north side of the valley on the way down.) However, the heroics proved unnecessary because by the time the troops reached Jamestown, the Dutch had already surrendered to Munden's naval attack.

In view of the successful British landing it is surprising that Prosperous Bay was not better fortified, but a survey by Governor Pyke in 1734, which consisted of rolling boulders down the side of the valley, concluded that fortification was unnecessary, putting into perspective the achievement of the British landing 60 years earlier. Nevertheless small batteries were installed later on and their ruins together with that of an old guardhouse remain.

Swimming is usually safe and there are good views of Turks Cap. It is also possible to walk eastward round the beach towards Bay Point. The familiar wave-cut platform and dykes (Walk 12a) gives rise to small pools and spectacular breakers. It was here that Keigwin made his landing.

The return is by the outward route; because the starting point was relatively low the walk is not too strenuous and can be done in an hour or so.

8 Sharks Valley

Elevation range: 430m – sea level
Length: 3.5km each way

Sharks Valley probably derives its name from the mackerel sharks that are fairly common on the windward side of the island, or it may be from the place where 'shirkers' would hide. The walk starts from the end of the tarmac road at Silver Hill. A wide path descends the back of a spur to a picnic table on the edge of an eroded area. When wet, these hummocky areas are extremely slippery with clinging mud. They are formed by the erosion of clay that has been disaggregated by the presence of sodium, so that water cannot penetrate. Even after heavy rain, when the top is a morass, the soil is dry just below the surface.

On the left is Warrens Gut and in it lies Hancock Hole spring, one of the island's best, which gives the valley its permanent stream – a feature that makes this walk so attractive. The high cost of pumping the water has prevented the spring's use for water supplies. The hole is named after Richard Hancock, a member of the failed Dennison rebellion of 1684, who remained a fugitive for 22 months using the hole as his hideout.

The path winds down the cliff at the end of the spur to the wooded valley bottom, where it crosses the stream for the first time. Emerging from the wood the path follows the left side of the valley, about 50m above the stream. This section needs caution. At one point the path splits into an upper and lower route ending at the same place; the lower route is slightly easier. The path then drops back to the valley floor with the towering canyon walls on either side. The route now criss-crosses the stream, passing through luxuriant growth of yams and wild mango. With their heart-shaped leaves, yams are common in many guts; they used to be cultivated for their edible roots and the plant was of such

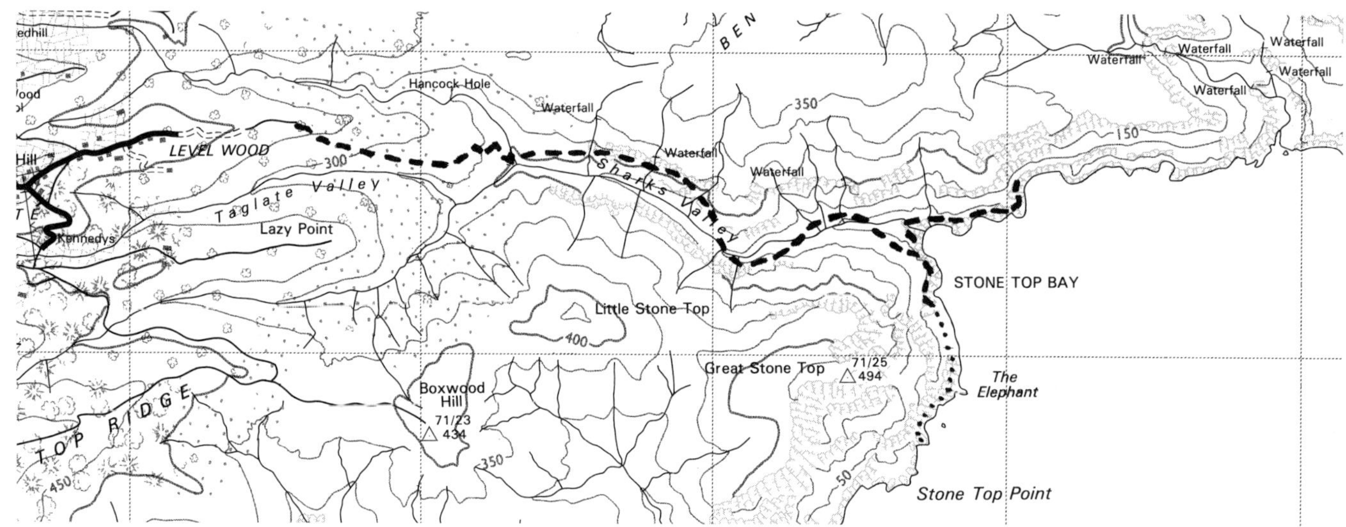

importance that islanders were known as 'Yamstocks'. Also common in this valley (and many others) is wild celery, which is edible but tough, and the ginger lily, similar to the plant from whose roots the spice is obtained, but in this case inedible.

Sharks Valley was never fortified. The absence of a landing place meant that fortifications at the seaward end of the valley were unnecessary. The remains of dry stone walling on the south canyon wall may be part of livestock fencing arrangements built by Hemmon Senior, a reclusive inhabitant of the valley in the 17th century.

There are several waterfalls before the final descent down a small, easily climbed cliff. Although not quite at sea level this spot offers a flat sandy area with running water that is ideal for camping. A scramble to the beach below is likely to yield driftwood and the waterfall provides a natural shower. Swimming off the beach is not possible as the sea is usually rough on this side of the island. However, a scramble along the rocks to the left towards Shore Island (George Island is straight ahead) leads to a wave-cut platform with a rock pool the size of a small swimming pool. This is a good picnic spot with an excellent view of Great Stone Top Cliff – at over 400m, the highest vertical fall on St Helena. Patches of vegetation clinging to the cliffs are watered by small springs that drip down on to the beach throughout the year (Walk 2).

Shore and George Islands are the only known breeding sites on St Helena of the masked booby and the brown booby. The nesting of both these tropical gannets was confirmed here only as recently as 1988. The masked booby is a large white seabird with black wingtips and tail and a blue-black patch surrounding the eyes. Its spectacular vertical plunge-dives in pursuit of fish aid identification at a distance. The brown booby is somewhat smaller and has a neat appearance with rich chocolate-brown upperparts sharply demarcated from the gleaming white. The large bill is banana-yellow. Boobies received their name somewhat unfairly because they are so frequently robbed of their food by frigate birds.

Before the descent down the last cliff to the camping beach a path leads off to the right, to the Elephant Rock and Great Stone Top Point – popular with the Levelwood fishermen. The path is only for confident walkers. Off this route an old path is supposed to lead back up the cliff to Great Stone Top but it doesn't appear to be used any more, even by fishermen. The return route is back up the valley with the stream offering refreshment for much of the way. The climb takes about an hour.

9 Bellstone – Great Stone Top

Elevation range: 540 – 380 – 500m
Length: 4km each way

This is a high-level walk through eroded country which ends with spectacular views from Little and Great Stone Top. A car can be left at the end of the tarmac on the road to Bellstone.

The Bellstone can be seen above the path to the right. It is the remains of a phonolitic column that would ring when struck (*phonos* means sound in Greek). The structure is the same as Lot and Lot's Wife. Unfortunately the rock has been damaged and has lost much of its ring.

The walk descends steeply through scrubby vegetation, mainly of Port Jackson willow. This area is frequented by flocks of Swainson's canary, an introduced southern African species. This is the finest songster on St Helena. The male is a handsome bird with streaked green upper parts and a yellow breast, belly and band above the eyes. Females are drab, streaky grey-green birds which can be distinguished from female and non-breeding male cardinals (Walk 23) by their short, stubby bill. Canaries are found throughout the island and often flock with waxbills (Walk 19).

As the vegetation thins the eroded country described in the Sharks Valley walk (Walk 8) predominates. Trench digging has been undertaken in some of the worst gullies in an attempt to stop erosion and encourage regeneration. Aloes have been planted to start this process; once some soil has accumulated, other species, such as Port Jackson willow, are planted.

The path crosses a saddle and Boxwood Hill lies directly ahead. Boxwood, an endemic shrub growing up to two metres high, was found mainly in this area until the early 19th century; however, it is now extinct. While the naturalist W.J. Burchell was the island's botanist and schoolmaster (1805-10), he recorded both scrubwood

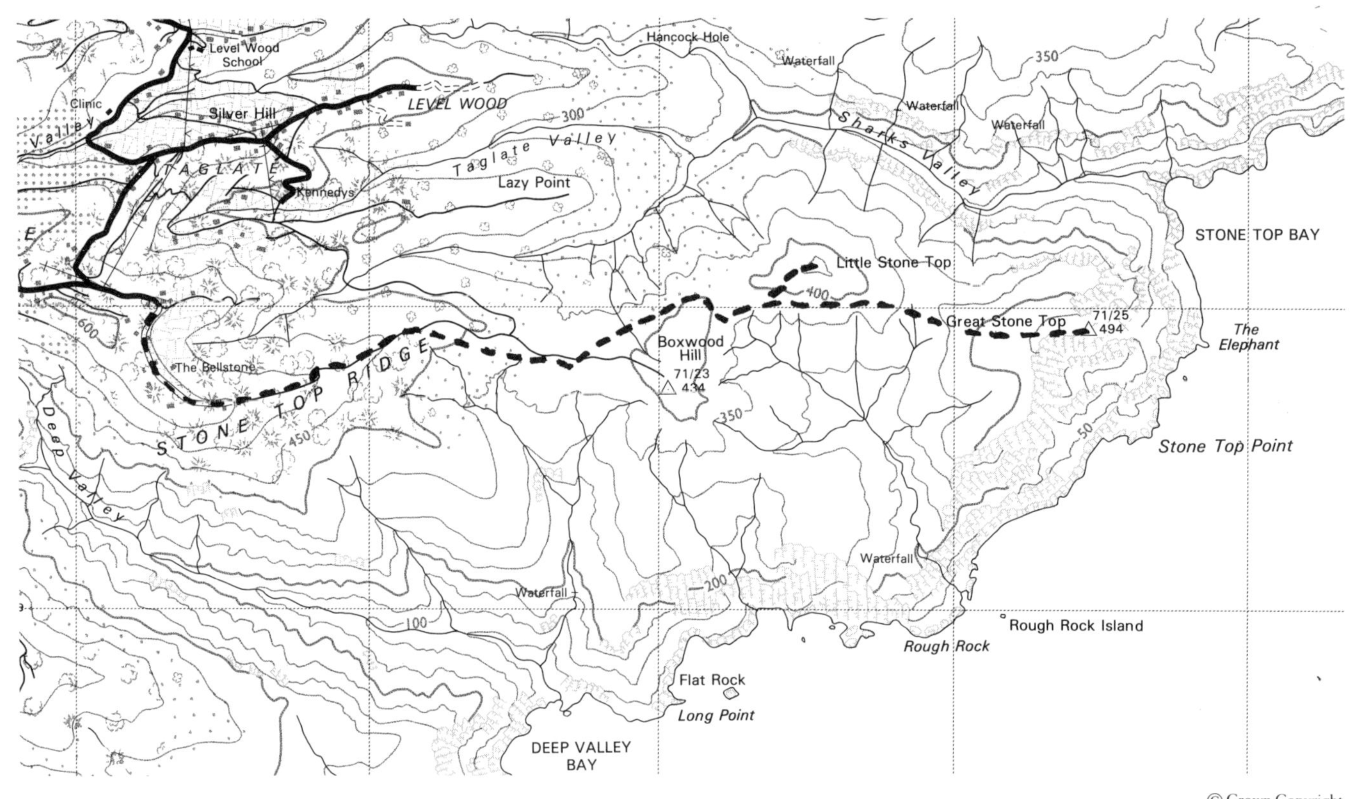

Level Wood School
Hancock Hole
Waterfall
350
Clinic
Valley
Silver Hill
LEVEL WOOD
300
Waterfall
Waterfall
Sharks Valley
Taglate Valley
TAGLATE
Lazy Point
Kennedys
STONE TOP BAY
Little Stone Top
400
Great Stone Top
71/25
494
The Elephant
600
Boxwood Hill
71/23
434
The Bellstone
STONE TOP RIDGE
350
Deep Valley
450
Stone Top Point
50
Waterfall
Waterfall
200
100
Rough Rock Island
Rough Rock
Flat Rock
Long Point
DEEP VALLEY BAY

and boxwood between Bellstone and Boxwood Hill, but by then most of the damage had been done. He noted that 'the soldiers and inhabitants have been suffered barbarianlike to cut down the trees with a wanton waste'.

Just before the ascent up Boxwood Hill the path forks to the right towards Deep Valley. (Access to Deep Valley by this route is extremely dangerous and should not be attempted. Levelwood fishermen use a path that takes off from near Bellstone to reach Deep Valley beach for fishing.) The climb to the top of Boxwood Hill is not particularly rewarding and can be avoided by taking a path to the left that skirts around the hill on the contour. However, the path has been partly eroded and, being above a steep drop, might present difficulties for some people.

The two Stone Tops represent some of the younger volcanic rocks on the island. They are composed of trachyte (as opposed to basalt over much of St Helena), which flows much less easily than basalt because of its high viscosity. The lava therefore has remained concentrated near the points of eruption, giving rise to the two hills.

The ascent up both the Stone Tops is relatively straightforward. From Little Stone Top there are excellent views down Sharks Valley and across Stone Top Bay. For those daring enough to peer over the edge of Great Stone Top Cliff the reward is a vertical drop of over 400m down St Helena's highest cliff.

The return journey is by the outward route, taking about an hour.

10 Rock Rose – Powell's Valley – Green Hill

Elevation range: 550m – sea level
Length: 2km down and 3.5km return

A full day should be set aside for this walk and it is advisable to be accompanied by someone who knows the route. Take plenty of liquid for the long haul back up, and a rope to help with a steep part of the walk. A second car parked at Green Hill saves the long walk back to Rock Rose.

Gabriel Powell was an early settler who landed with Keigwin in 1673 (see Walk 7). A descendant of his, George Gabriel Powell, was Acting Governor in 1742-4. The Powell family owned land at the head of the valley near Green Hill. The entrance to the drive of Rock Rose is marked by a large Norfolk Island pine which is the largest tree on the island and thought to be at least 200 years old. It is used as a landmark by fishermen. The house dates from the early 18th century but its history is obscure. Early in his captivity Napoleon, escorted by Bertrand, gave his British escort, Poppleton, the slip and galloped to Rock Rose (then lived in by R. Seale, famed for the model he made of the island and also for his *Geognosy*) and beyond to the ridge dividing Deep and Powell's Valleys. Did Napoleon seriously contemplate escape via Powell's which was unguarded at the time? Although he returned peaceably to Longwood, the British fears of their prisoner escaping were fuelled by this incident and Napoleon was subsequently guarded much more closely. The remains of an old flax mill (see Walk 21) lie near the house – a good picnic spot (see Other Walks).

The route starts by following the track that runs to the side of Rock Rose and continues out to Long Range (it is an easy but not particularly interesting walk to Long Range Point). The path to Powell's Valley leads off from the track through some trees about 400m after leaving Rock Rose and follows the side of the cliff

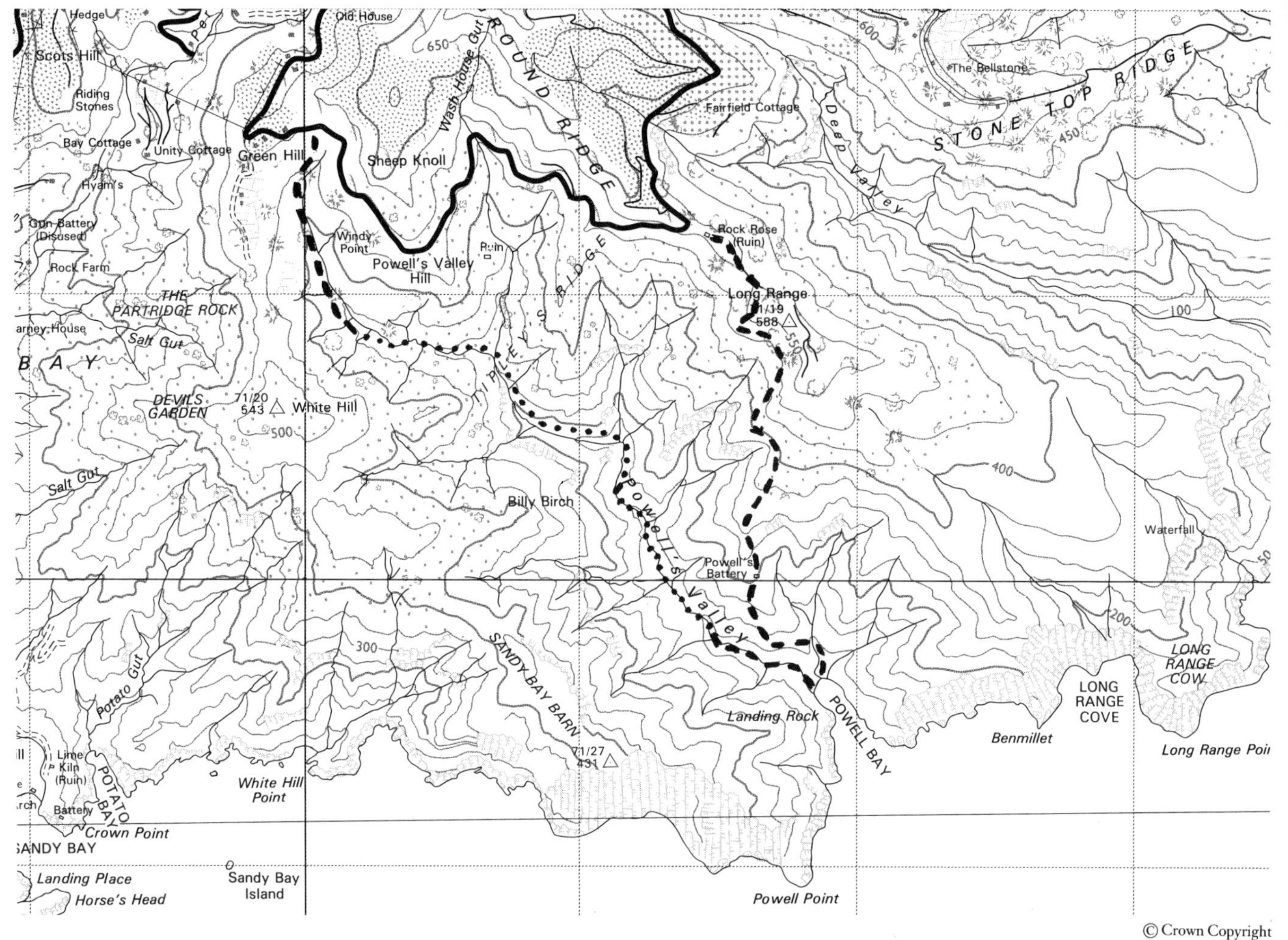
Hedge
Scots Hill
Riding Stones
Bay Cottage
Unity Cottage
Green Hill
Old House
650
Wash House Gut
ROUND RIDGE
Sheep Knoll
Fairfield Cottage
600
The Bellstone
STONE TOP RIDGE
450
Deep Valley
Hyam's
Gun Battery (Disused)
Rock Farm
Windy Point
Powell's Valley Hill
Ruin
Rock Rose (Ruin)
Long Range
588
550
THE PARTRIDGE ROCK
Salt Gut
B A Y
DEVILS GARDEN
71/20
543
White Hill
500
TIPLEY'S RIDGE
100
400
Salt Gut
Billy Birch
Powell's Valley
Powell's Battery
Waterfall
200
300
SANDY BAY BARN
Potato Gut
Lime Kiln (Ruin)
POTATO BAY
Battery
Crown Point
SANDY BAY
White Hill Point
71/27
431
Landing Rock
POWELL BAY
LONG RANGE COVE
LONG RANGE COW
Benmillet
Landing Place
Horse's Head
Sandy Bay Island
Powell Point

below Long Range. When viewed across the valley from Sandy Bay Barn this path looks hair-raising to say the least, but as is so often the case, the reality is less daunting with aloes and flax lining the path and providing a good barrier against any feelings of vertigo. The view of Sandy Bay Barn from this path is superb (Walk 11).

It is surprising that it was considered necessary to fortify such a steep valley as Powell's. Nevertheless Governor Patton thought a landing possible when he inspected the area in 1804, although it was still unfortified in 1816. The remains of the two batteries that command Powell Bay 300m below are possibly a direct result of Napoleon's visit. The path runs over the left-hand end of the right-hand battery and then starts a steep drop to the valley floor. There is a scramble at one point down a short steep incline where a rope is of assistance. From here it is a short distance to the beach. In wet weather there is a stream running in the valley which, although slightly saline, is quite drinkable. The beach area provides quite a good campsite.

The return is hard going since the start of the walk at Rock Rose was at 550m – one of the highest starts for a coastal path. The return can be either by the way down or by continuing back up the valley towards Green Hill. There is no path as such on the valley floor and in places the vegetation is fairly thick, so it is essential to be accompanied by someone who knows the route. Half-way along, the route is overlooked by Billy Birch Cliff (Walk 11). Care is needed to take the correct route (see map) following the main valley. At the end of the valley a low cliff has to be scaled so as to emerge into the upper reaches. From there the walk is straightforward up the valley bottom pastures, with a final steep scramble through the pine trees up to Green Hill.

11 Green Hill – Sandy Bay Barn

Elevation range: undulating 400 – 500m
Length: 2.5km out and 3.5km return

When he visited St Helena in 1836, Darwin thought that the Sandy Bay Basin was the remnant of the original volcanic crater, the other half of which had vanished into the sea. Subsequently it was found that the 'crater' was in fact an erosional feature due to the soft rock in the area. This walk follows the edge of the eastern edge of the 'crater' and offers some of the finest views on St Helena. In 1808 Thomas Brooke wrote, 'It would be difficult, perhaps, in any country to meet with a more uncommon and romantic prospect than Sandy Bay, when seen from many parts of the main ridge.'

A car can be left at the end of the little track running down from Green Hill. Adequate protection against sun and wind should be taken, as the walk runs along exposed ground. The path starts by running along the side of a flax hedge that is the boundary of the adjacent smallholding. The route then leads up to the summit of White Hill across eroded and exposed country. A short sharp ascent to the top of White Hill – appropriately named for its bald eroded appearance – and the full grandeur of the Sandy Bay Valley is apparent. Binoculars and a map are useful for picking out the detail on the other side of the valley. The path continues down the other side of White Hill and fairly clearly along the ridge crest towards Sandy Bay Barn; the views remain impressive.

Some of St Helena's most recent lava flows formed White Hill and Sandy Bay Barn, which geologically are quite distinct from the Barn. These later flows overlie older lava and the superimposition of the new over the old is clear in any distant view of Sandy Bay Barn (as from Walk 10).

The walk to the foot of the Sandy Bay Barn is easy. This is a

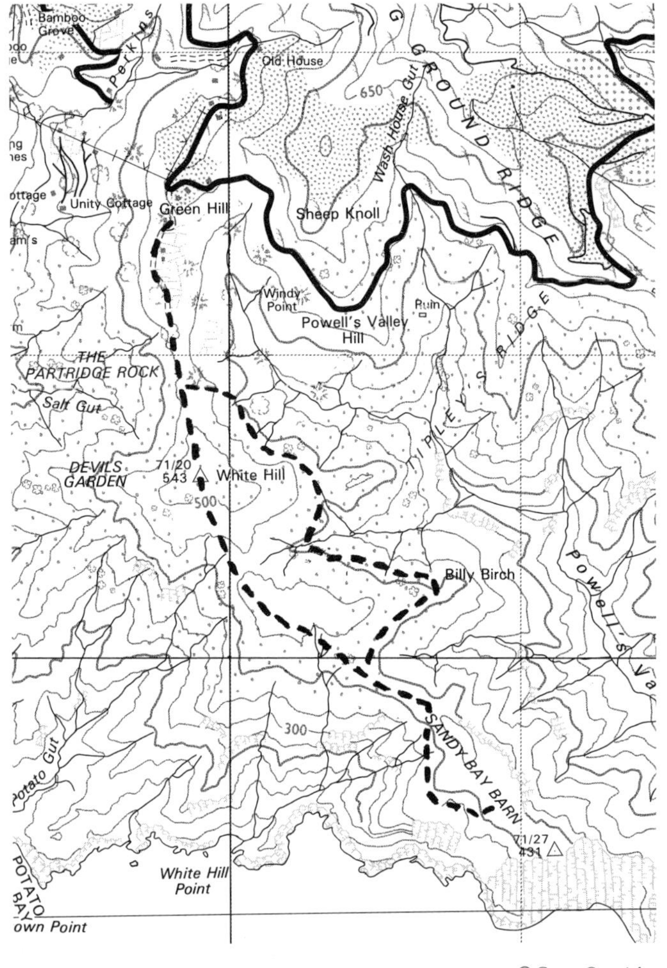

good spot for a picnic, with views over Powell's Valley. Getting on to Sandy Bay Barn itself is slightly more difficult. A scramble can be made up the rocks straight ahead, or a path of sorts leads off to the right, running under the mountain. The first 100-200m of this route are difficult, being on the side of a steep but vegetated slope with vertiginous drops below. Thereafter it is an easy climb to the top, where there is a surprisingly large, flat, mesembryanthemum-covered area. The southern end of the Sandy Bay Barn supports a massive cliff.

The return walk can be made by going around the east side of White Hill. Having returned to the base of the Barn and retraced the outward route for some 200-300m, the alternative path leads away to the right. From this path a small detour leads to Billy Birch Cliff over which, on 17 June 1693, young William Birch fell to his death while driving his goats.

From Billy Birch onwards the path is in a poor state, leading over heavily eroded and not particularly attractive countryside. It rejoins the main path on the north side of White Hill from where only a short walk remains back up to Green Hill.

12 Sandy Bay Beach – Lot's Wife Ponds

Elevation range: sea level – 220m
Length: 2.5km each way

This is one of St Helena's best known walks. It is quite manageable by small children and the Ponds themselves offer one of St Helena's most enjoyable stretches of coast. If there is time for only one coastal walk, this is the one to take. But remember to take a length of rope, sunscreen and plenty of liquid.

Cars are normally left on the flat ground just above Sandy Bay Beach (which used to be a parade ground), or at the top of the track leading down to it. The path starts on the hillside on the opposite side of Broad Gut and follows the right-hand side of a small valley running away from Sandy Bay. A guide is advisable since parts of the route are not always clear and straying off the path, even to take an apparent short cut, can be dangerous.

The path follows the valley to its head. Although totally barren at first glance, there are in fact some interesting plants to be seen along the way. Endemic baby's toes are low-growing succulents which exude water when crushed and are easily recognized; in hot weather they dry up, leaving grey skeletons on the ground. Ice plants, which are a type of mesembryanthemum, are also fairly common; they are covered by clear raised dots which make the plant look icy. Surprisingly, there are edible baby tomatoes that grow wild in the sides of some of the dried up guts.

At the end of the valley the path zigzags sharply up to a saddle that more or less marks half-way. The spectacular views from this point can be admired with the comforting knowledge that the path is mainly downhill from here on.

A few hundred metres after starting the descent a second saddle is reached, where the path splits. The route to the Ponds (the right fork) is marked by stones on the ground but the path to the left also looks to be in invitingly good order. In fact it leads to an area of white sand from where there is only a difficult and dangerous scramble to rejoin the main path.

The white sand deposits have fascinated visitors to this part of the island. Highly calcareous sand dunes are not a feature to be expected 150m above sea level. Their origins are the subject of debate. Some call them 'raised beaches' and cite them as evidence of sea-level changes, backed up by other features of apparent marine origin such as Prosperous Bay Plain (Walk 7). Others think that they were formed by wind blown from former offshore sand banks in the Benguela Current, and that they have survived in areas out of the wind. In any event they provided a valuable source of lime for building purposes. The path to the Ponds was originally constructed for mining the sand, which was taken back to the kiln in Sandy Bay Valley (Walk 12a).

The path ends at the top of a low cliff above the Ponds. Although this is fairly easily negotiated, a rope makes the descent much easier. Of the two possible routes down, the left is easier although it may not appear that way when looking from above. Immediately opposite this cliff stands an isolated pillar of rock, known as the Chimney, which is a dyke that has resisted the erosion that has removed the surrounding lava flows.

The Ponds are formed by a combination of the wave-cut platform (Walk 12a) and a long dyke that guards its outside edge from the sea. In most weather waves crash over the outside wall, thus ensuring that the water remains clean. However in calm weather the Ponds become stagnant and it is necessary to move farther eastward along the beach to find clean water for swimming. Although swimming in the Ponds is quite safe, it is extremely dangerous to climb on to the outside wall, as waves can crash over the outer wall unexpectedly. During the past few years several people who have ignored warnings have been injured.

For more intrepid explorers one of the joys of Lot's Wife Ponds

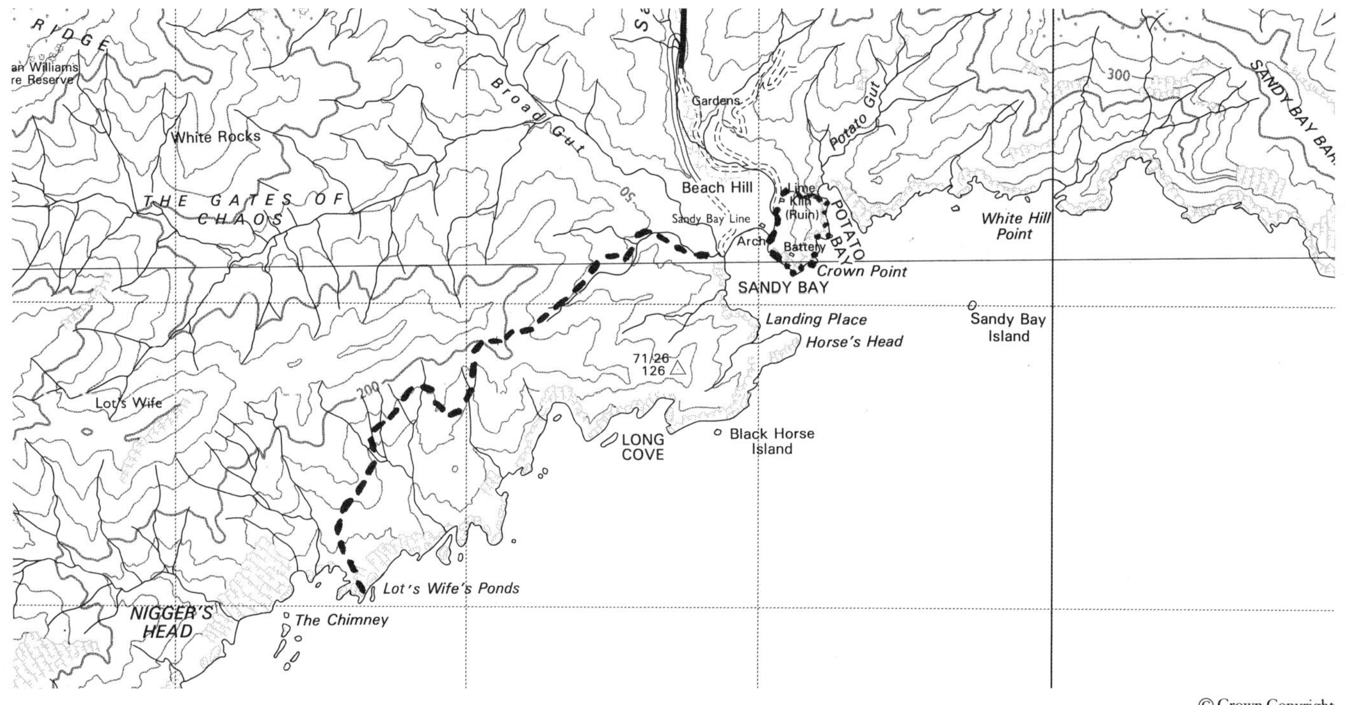

is the walk along the coast westwards. This involves one or two carefully timed leaps and edging along a cliff face helped by a none-too-safe wire, installed by fishermen, before the beach terminates in a sheer drop after about a kilometre. Small blow holes in the lava and a large inland cave still connected to the sea add to the interest.

The Ponds offer an attractive campside but there is no fresh water and very little driftwood, so these have to be brought in. Do not underestimate the amount of liquid required. The walk back can normally be completed in about an hour, since there is less to carry than on the way out.

Sandy Bay Lines. (Burchell)

Sandy Bay Lines from Broad Gut. (Burchell)

12a Sandy Bay Beach – Potato Bay

Elevation range: sea level – 50m
Length: 0.8km round trip

This short walk provides an interesting addition to the Lot's Wife Ponds walk or a separate destination for a seaside picnic. The walk only takes about half an hour each way.

Cars can be parked just above Sandy Bay Beach (see Walk 12). The walk starts a few metres back up Sandy Bay Gut. The gut can be reached either by going around the beach under the arch of the old fortification (which may require a leap to avoid getting wet feet), or by going up over Beach Hill between Broad Gut and Sandy Bay Gut; this latter route offers the chance to inspect the old battery on the hill top.

The path to Potato Bay (the origin of the name remains a mystery) takes off up the cliff by the ruins of an old lime kiln. The kiln was used to produce lime for building from the calcareous sand mined in the area (Walk 12). It was the firing of this kiln, and possibly others like it that have disappeared, that probably caused the near extinction of the St Helena ebony that in the 17th century was common in the Sandy Bay area (Walk 20 describes where and when it was rediscovered). The combination of man – cutting trees down for firewood – and goats led to the extinction of many of St Helena's endemic trees and shrubs by the end of the 19th century.

The path winds sharply up to the hill crest and is very loose in places. It then drops down sharply on the other side to Potato Bay. Although short, this walk needs some care. The bay offers swimming in calm weather.

The return can be made by the outward walk but in calm weather it is more interesting to continue around the wave-cut platform on the west side of the bay (this route is for more intrepid walkers who don't mind getting wet). A wave-cut platform

Potato Bay from Crown Point. (Burchell)

Potato Bay. (Burchell)

surrounds much of St Helena's coastline; the platform is situated between three and six metres above current sea level and, with attendant dry caves, points to a fairly recent higher sea level. The route over the platform at Potato Bay is not feasible in rough weather but otherwise is very pleasant. It ends at the foot of a low cliff which provides a fairly easy climb to the top where there is a well defined path leading back to Sandy Bay Valley. An old battery is passed on the way. There is a good view of the Sandy Bay fortifications from this route.

The main fortifications at Sandy Bay are the work of Governor Lambert and were erected in 1742. He designed both the platforms at the mouths of Broad Gut and Sandy Bay Valley and the adjoining wall, thus making one continuous line. Unfortunately his decision to speed up construction by not using mortar gave the wall a short life and the western section has long since vanished. Further fortifications were placed at Horse's Head and Seale's Battery but these, along with the main line, are rapidly deteriorating ruins.

On the way home, as the road starts to wind up the hill to Bamboo Hedge, you pass Jenkins Cottage on the left. This was the residence of Governor Jenkins (1740-42) of Ear War fame. Earlier in his career in the West Indies he was attacked by Spaniards who cut off his ear. Upon returning to England he exhibited his torn ear before the House of Commons and when asked of his feelings about the event made the memorable reply 'I committed my soul to God and my cause to my country'. An incensed House promptly declared war on Spain.

13 Botleys – Manati Bay

Elevation range: 550m – sea level
Length: 2.5km each way

This walk requires considerable stamina on the return journey and – while offering pleasant views – can safely be placed as a low priority. Along with the walks to Powell's Valley (Walk 10) and Thompson's Valley (Walk 14), the 550m climb back up means that it is not a particularly good walk for children. A full day should be set aside for the walk. Take a length of rope and plenty to drink.

Manati Bay derives its name from the alternative word for sea cow, but this is a misdescription for what appear to have been elephant seals. Manatees/sea cows/dugongs are mammals that feed in shallow water and are thought to have given rise to the legend of mermaids. However, the deep waters around St Helena are quite unsuitable for their survival. Instead it is likely that the southern elephant seal, which is generally found farther south in much colder waters, lies behind the name. In 1656 an English seaman, Peter Mundy, described a 'manatee' as having 'the coullor (yellowish) and terrible countenance of a lion, with four greatt teeth, besides smalle, longe, bigge, smelling haires or mustaches … in length aboutt ten foote and five foote aboutt the middle'.

In the 18th century these animals were occasionally found on the beaches on the southern side of the island and killed for their oil. Their subsequent destruction by commercial sealers operating in the Southern Ocean has meant that none have been reported on St Helena since 1819; however, with the cessation of sealing, numbers are recovering fast and the possibility of further sitings on St Helena's southern shores cannot be ruled out.

The walk starts at Botleys. Having crossed the fence that marks the lower edge of Botleys pastures, the path winds down steeply through a rapid change in vegetation. The fence marks the

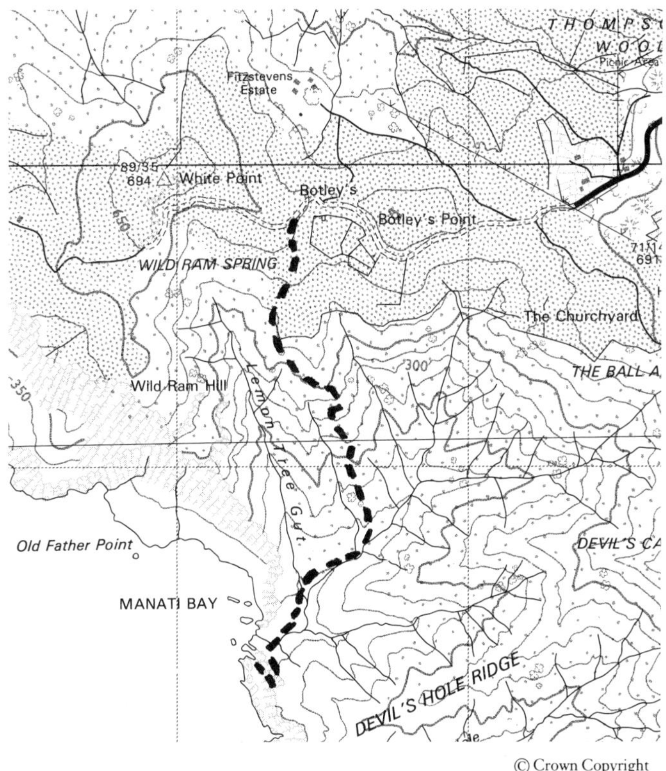

boundary of the Crown Waste. About two-thirds of the island is classified as Crown Waste. It is a loosely used term to describe the barren land on the periphery of the island where rainfall is low and erosion has been severe. The Crown Waste is now administratively defined and attempts are being made to reclaim the more promising areas. In order to preserve the vegetation, sheep and goats that stray from the neighbouring pastures are shot by the Government; wild rabbits still abound, however.

The lower part of the walk follows the course of Manati Bay Stream which at its lower end falls to the beach below. Through much of the year the stream supports a small trickle, although the water is quite saline in the lower reaches. It is necessary to cross the steam and climb the hill on the other side, as clambering down the waterfall is not recommended (however, since this is the only route on to the beach, it must be followed if that is the destination). Having climbed the hill, getting down the other side is considerably easier with a rope. This route gives access to the wave-cut platform to the south of Manati Bay; it is possible to walk along the platform for some distance and there are one or two very small pools that offer the chance of a dip (but not a swim) on a hot day.

The return journey is a long hard climb by the downward route, taking about an hour and a half. A cold drink, left in the car, goes down very well after such exertion.

14 Thompson's Valley

Elevation range: 550m – sea level
Length: 3.2km each way

This is another walk which starts at a high level, thus presenting a hard climb on the return journey, but there is plenty of interest to see along the way. The origin of the name Thompson appears to be a corruption of tombstone (spelled tomstone), a name applied to the area of boulders littering the grass at the head of the valley. A similar feature on the other side of Hooper's Ridge is still known as the Churchyard.

The start of the path is not very clear and it is advisable to have a guide to point it out. Initially the walk is through pine forest before emerging on the hillside by High Hill House. Lush vegetation reduces any feelings of vertigo at this point as the path winds across a couple of springs and around the side of the valley with High Hill rising abruptly overhead. There are fine views both down the valley and across to Man and Horse Pastures.

This area provides a good opportunity to see one of St Helena's introduced gamebirds, the chukar partridge. Even if the bird itself remains hidden, there is a good chance that its harsh, cackling call will be heard among the rocks. Chukars were brought to St Helena from the Middle East by the Portuguese in the 16th century and soon became abundant. Regular hunting has since reduced their numbers but they still remain relatively common in the more arid parts of the island, though they are secretive and wary. The chukar is about the size of a domestic bantam with buffish-grey upperparts, scarlet bill and legs and a black stripe across the eyes which extends to the sides of the neck and across the breast to form a broad 'necklace'. The paler underparts are barred with black and chestnut on the flanks.

About a kilometre after the start the path crosses a ridge and

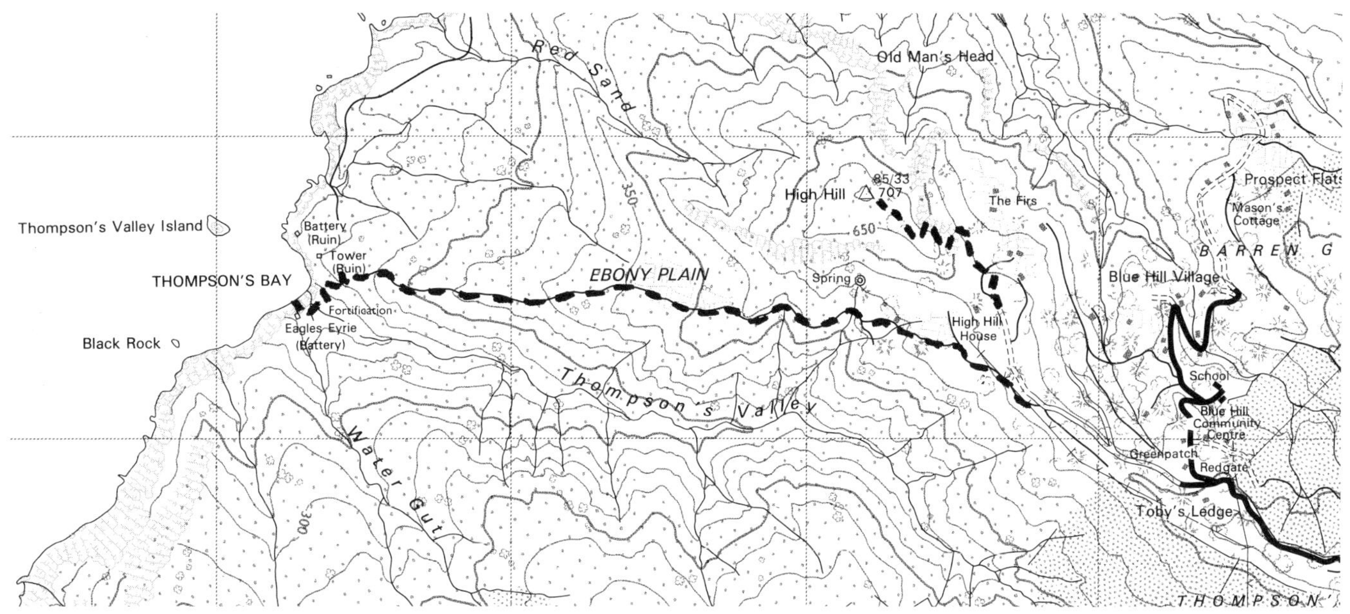

turns to the right, away from the side of the valley to cross Ebony Plain. Ebony Plain is the site of a major effort to re-establish the endemic ebony tree (see Walk 20). Previously the area was covered by prickly pear but this has been windrowed and the ebonies planted in the clearing. The plants are at their best during the winter months (when there is more rainfall), but can flower at any time of the year.

At the end of the Plain the land starts to slope more steeply and the vegetation gives way to the barren expanses of the Dry Zone. There are good views over the ocean and schools of dolphin and the shadows of shoals of fish can often be seen. The path continues almost to the edge of the cliff before starting to wind down the valley side. Before descending into the valley it is worth inspecting the ruins of the old guard tower situated about 100m below the start of the downward path. Farther on, some way below the tower, is a battery, which is easily accessible. (However, it is not possible to reach the beach this way.) The battery commands a fine position dominating the approaches to Thompson's Bay and, combined with another battery at Eagle's Eyrie on the other side of the valley and the wall at the mouth of the valley, makes a formidable obstacle to any would-be attacker.

It is necessary to return above the tower to start the walk down

Egg Island. (Burchell)

into the valley. The route needs some care as the path is slippery and not well used. The fortified wall across the face of the valley is well preserved but can be easily negotiated. Swimming from the beach is usually safe, although the large and slippery boulders make entry and exit potentially hazardous.

A long hard climb by the downward route is the only way back.

15 Sarah's Valley – Lemon Valley

Elevation range: 450m – sea level
Length: 2.5km each way

Lemon Valley beach is the nearest that St Helena has to a holiday resort and so can become relatively crowded at weekends and during holiday periods. A pleasant way to visit the beach is to walk down and arrange, prior to departure, for a boat to pick the party up later in the day for transport back to Jamestown. (Alternatively, for non-walkers, the journey can be made by boat both ways.)

Lemon Valley is largely responsible for the stories of St Helena's great former abundance. Lemons were introduced in 1718 and thrived at first but later pests and diseases became established and uncontrollable (partly because there are so few natural predators on the island). The appearance of lemon trees in the lower reaches of this lush valley must have reminded early sailors of the Garden of Eden – particularly after a long hard voyage. Given that they probably did not have easy access to other parts of the island the fertility of this little spot was undoubtedly given much greater prominence than it really deserved.

To reach the start of the path you have to drive to Rosemary Plain, considered to be one of the best parts of the island in which to live. Rosemary Hall, now demolished, was one of St Helena's great houses and was offered by Hudson Lowe as an alternative to Longwood as Napoleon's residence. The path begins at Crack Plain and follows the side of Sarah's Valley. At its upper levels vegetation is thick, but this soon gives way to scrub and eventually to prickly pear. The walk is pleasant if unremarkable. After about 20 minutes the appropriately shaped Friar's Rock appears high overhead at the top of Friar's Ridge on the right-hand side of the path. One story goes that a Roman Catholic chapel stood in Friar's Valley and that the resident friar fell in love with a girl tending her

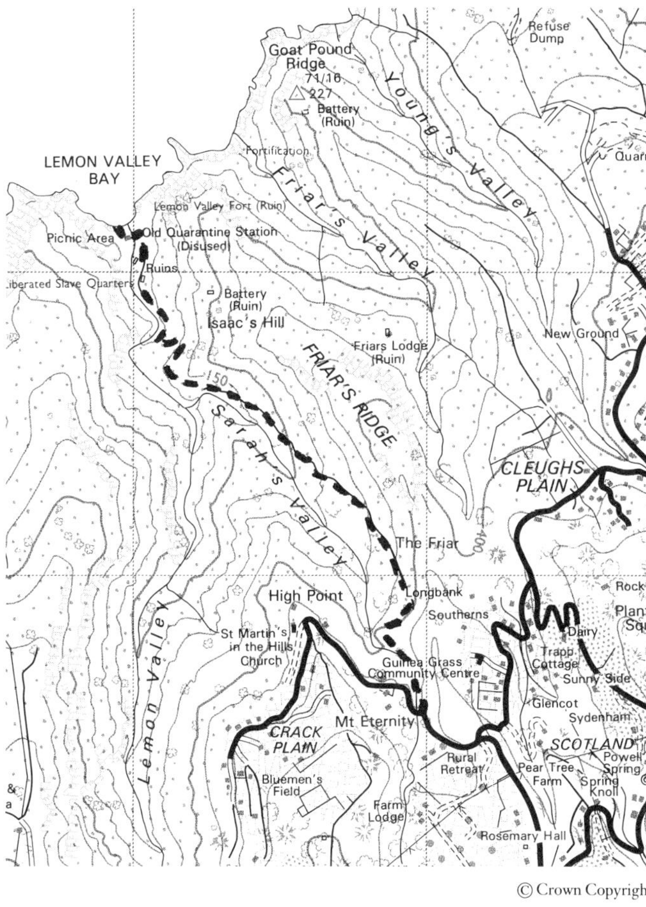

goats on nearby Goat Pound Ridge. She agreed to marry him on the condition that he renounce his Catholicism. Finally in desperation he agreed. On the day of the marriage, as they held hands at the altar, there was a fearful 'crack' and the girl was swallowed up by the earth and the friar turned to stone. Presumably the nearby Crack Plain was the site of this disaster.

The path is fairly slippery in places due to loose gravel and care is needed. About two kilometres from the start, Sarah's Valley joins Lemon Valley proper coming in from the left. The path winds around a rock bluff and then zigzags down a loose bouldery slope to the valley bottom. It is then a short walk down the valley, under the fortified arch and on to the beach. On the way to the beach are a number of ruins that were used as a secondary depot for slaves released from intercepted ships during the mid-19th century (see Walk 3).

Lemon Valley Bay with its surrounding fortifications is a most attractive stretch of coastline. The ascent to Half Moon Battery, perched on the cliffs on the west side of the bay, is easy and gives good views back across the bay towards Jamestown. On the way up there is a magazine in good condition, but a torch is needed to explore it. The Dutch landed here in December 1672 but were foiled by the English defenders hurling down boulders from the precipices above. The Dutch withdrew only to make a successful landing at Old Woman's Valley on New Year's Day 1673. The fortification of Lemon Valley started soon after the English recaptured the island in May of the same year (see Walk 7), and today the fort is one of the best preserved on St Helena. The guard house remains almost intact and the ruins of the old quarantine station lie up the valley. The site was used for quarantine purposes as far back as 1717 for slaves from Madagascar infected with smallpox and, more recently, for the last batch of Boer prisoners, who had been exposed to bubonic plague in Cape Town.

Recently the beach area has been upgraded. The stream has

been tapped to provide a piped water supply, latrines installed, trees planted and the coastline tidied up. Swimming is excellent throughout the year. Swimmers are often surprised that immediately after entering the water from the beach they encounter a sandy bottom – almost unique for the island. The cave and the buildings offer overnight accommodation, while the landing rocks allow both good swimming and an easy embarkation for a boat trip home.

View of Jamestown from the road leading to the Briars. (G. W. Melliss)

Jamestown from Ladder Hill

Vue de Sommet de Ladder Hill from a painting by Durand Brager, 1844

Seale's Bridge. (Burchell)

Rupert's Bay from Sampson's Battery. (David Bentham)

Wirebird chick. (Neil McCulloch)

Banks Battery. (Dave Bentham)

Prosperous Bay and the Barn. (Dave Bentham)

Green Hill and White Hill. (Dave Bentham)

Little Stone Top. (Burchell)

Sandy Bay. (Dave Bentham)

Manati Bay. (Dave Bentham)

On the walk to Manati Bay. (Dave Bentham)

Near Half Moon Battery, Lemon Valley

The local charabanc – for leisurely picnics

Ebonies and Lot's wife. (Dave Bentham)

Tree ferns and Flagstaff. (Dave Bentham)

Speery Island from Man and Horse

Napoleon's tomb

Inland Walks

Willow Cottage. (G. W. Melliss)

16 Briars – Barnes Road – Francis Plain

Elevation range: 280 – 450m
Length: 2km

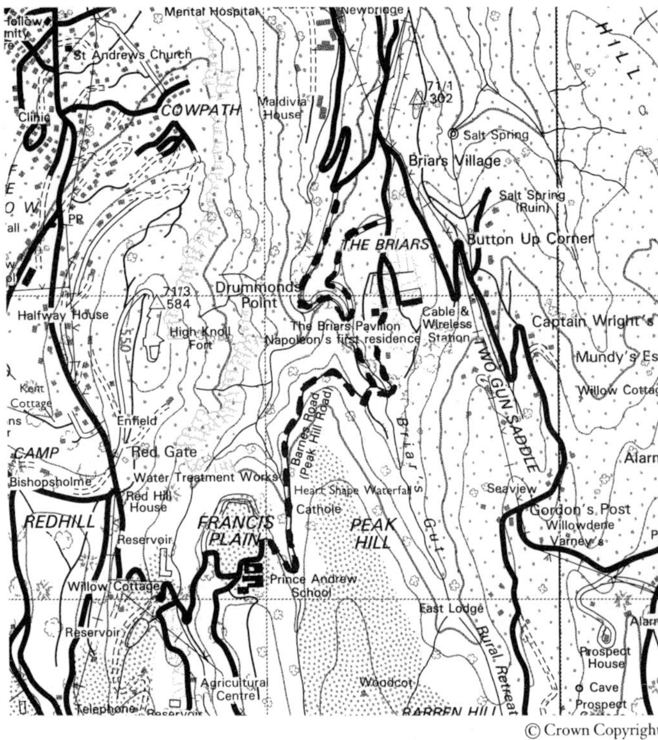

This is a short walk, of historical interest, that you can make in both directions or incorporate as part of a walk from Jamestown to Francis Plain – a route taken by children who miss the school bus.

The Briars was Napoleon's residence for the first two months of his captivity in 1815. Following a visit to Longwood to see his quarters in preparation, he was returning reluctantly to Jamestown when he saw the Briars below. The owner, Mr Balcombe offered, as he would have done to any visiting dignitary, the Pavilion as Napoleon's temporary residence. The time that the Emperor spent at the Briars and his relationship with Balcombe's daughter Betsy is well described by Dame Mabel Brookes in *St Helena Story* (1960). Today the building, together with Longwood House, is a museum containing memorabilia from Napoleon's stay. An historical coincidence is that Wellington also spent a few days at the Briars on his return from India in 1805; he commented on this in a letter to Admiral Malcolm, commander of the St Helena forces in 1816, in which he asked Malcolm to tell 'Bony' that 'I find his apartments at the Elysée Bourbon very convenient, and I hope he likes mine at Mr Balcom's'. Perhaps not surprisingly there is no mention of this story in the French-owned building.

The Barnes Road takes its name from a Major Barnes who supervised prisoners and liberated slaves in constructing the road in the mid-19th century. The walk starts at the track that turns right at the red gate posts marking the entrance to the Balcombes' former driveway. (The main house has been demolished and the garden is now used by Cable and Wireless.) After a few hundred metres the track makes a hairpin turn to the right and the path leads off to the left, over Black Bridge. An alternative walk can be made to the base of the Heart Shape Waterfall by continuing down the track to the next sharp bend at Drummonds Point (see Other Walks). Back at Black Bridge, the path begins its winding ascent of Peak Hill via Barnes Road; before long an alternative route back to the Briars is offered by a path off to the left that descends and crosses Briars Gut. Following the upward path the spur of Peak Hill is rounded and there are excellent views down James Valley.

From here the path continues into the lower reaches of Lemon Tree Gut before making the final ascent to Francis Plain.

The wooded valley below the Briars is a roosting site for common mynahs. Hundreds of these vociferous birds gather here

'Some of the dangers of cricket on the Plain: "Jack's gone over the cliff".' (Graphic 1886)

at sunset and the noise near the roost can be quite deafening. The mynah is chocolate-brown with black head, breast and tail. The bill, legs and bare skin round the eyes are orange-yellow. In flight large white patches on the wings allow easy identification. The mynah has an extraordinary vocal repertoire, ranging from harsh squawks to thrush-like warbles. The present population is descended from five birds from India liberated by Miss Phoebe Moss from her home at the Briars in 1885 in order to control cattle ticks. Mynahs are highly adaptable birds and, in the absence of effective predators, have been able to exploit all manner of food sources, including fruit crops, to such a degree that their numbers have reached pest proportions.

Francis Plain is named after Henry Francis who owned the land in 1692. It was used as one of the principal camping grounds during Napoleon's captivity and is now St Helena's main public recreation ground. The pavilion was built in 1925 in honour of the last Governor to die on the island – Governor Peel. The plain was levelled in the 1970s and all the island's football and cricket fixtures are played here. About one in ten of the active male population plays cricket. Before its expansion to its present shape the plain was rather small for a game of cricket and an unfortunate fieldsman fell to his death in the 1880s, while chasing a ball over the steep hill into the valley.

The Prince Andrew School overlooks the plain and is the island's only upper school; its inception was announced by Prince Andrew during his visit and it was opened in 1989. Incorporated into the building is Francis Plain House, used to accommodate another of St Helena's political prisoners – the Zulu chief Dinizulu who was held on the island between 1890-97. Just to the side of the school is Olive Cottage, formerly a gaming house for officers, dating from about 1823.

From Francis Plain it is a quick walk downhill back to the Briars, particularly if the short cut across Briars Gut is taken.

17 Oakbank – Bates Branch – White Gate

Elevation range: undulating 500 – 675m
Length: 3.5km

As with other circular walks, there are several possible starting points for this walk. Probably the easiest is to start at White Gate where there is space to leave cars. From here take the road down towards Knollcombes (see Other Walks) through the avenue of thorn trees. These trees, otherwise known as Kaffir Booms, were originally imported from South Africa. Their thorny trunks make them resistant to damage from grazing animals, although their foliage provides excellent fodder. Consequently they can be seen marking field and estate boundaries all over the island. They have spectacular red blooms in winter and their seeds are used for bead work.

The wooded roadsides in the centre of the island are favourite feeding sites for the delicate little barred ground dove (known locally as turtle dove). Small flocks of up to a dozen are frequently encountered picking up fallen seeds on the road. This species is a native of south-east Asia and Australia and was probably introduced in the early 18th century. The dove is dusty cinnamon above with blue-grey face and underparts. Darker margins to the feathers give a scaly appearance. Ground doves are common around human habitation where they may become very tame, as in the Public Gardens in Jamestown.

Shortly after the path to the Boer Cemetery (which is worth a diversion), take the right-hand track that leads to Oakbank. Follow the track through woodland for about 400m until a sharp U bend is reached. Oakbank is privately owned by the Thorpe family. The house is one of the oldest on the island, being mentioned in the records for 1684. It was the home of G. W. Mellis until 1840 and then of the first two Bishops of St Helena, from 1859 to 1878

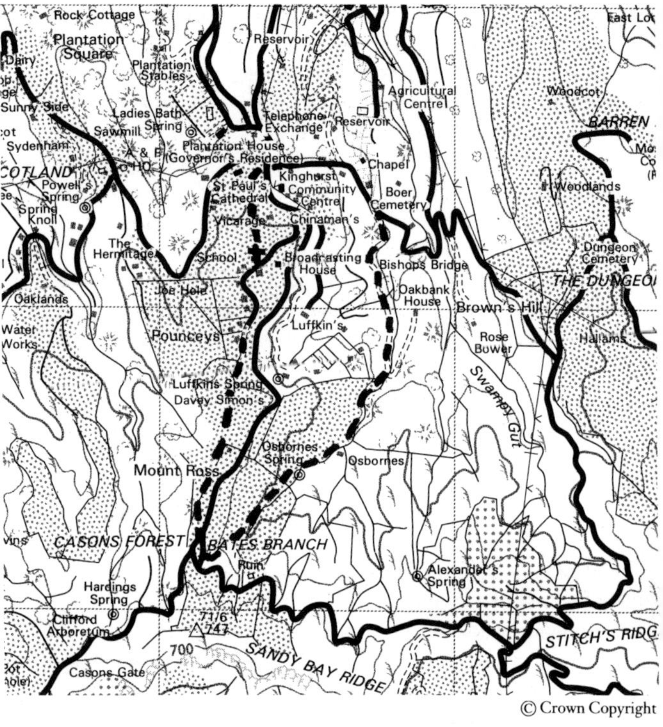

(hence Bishops Bridge just below Oakbank), and remained Church property until sold for £750 in 1899, dilapidated by white-ant. In January 1899 Bishop Welby, who lived in the house at the time, was killed in a pony and trap accident on Shy Road – his ghost is still said to haunt the house.

From the U bend there is a path doubling back to the right through the flax which eventually emerges on to pastures above Oakbank. A track leads up the valley past Osborne's Cottage and the collection system for Osborne's Spring that supplies water to Redhill treatment works (the large green tank on the crest of the hill above Francis Plain). Gorse is common in this area and on much of St Helena's pastures and is difficult to eradicate; originally introduced as a fuel plant, it is still used as such in the ovens of a few country cottages. Kikuyu grass is the predominant pasture grass on the island, although it was introduced only in 1934. It sends out long stolons and eliminates most competition including the formerly common 'hay' grasses.

A barbed wire fence marks the end of the Osborne pastures and from this point take a straight line up the hill to the right, over the adjacent pasture to Bates Branch road junction. Cross the road to the old bus shelter and turn on to a path that runs parallel to the main road back to White Gate but above it. After a short walk through woodland (look out for raspberries here, if they are in season), another fence has to be climbed before reaching the open pasture land of Mount Ross. The origin of this name is not clear but may be related to the polar explorer James Clark Ross, whose expedition to the Antarctic called at St Helena in 1839 and 1843 (see Walk 25). More probably it is named after Governor Sir Patrick Ross (1846-50).

From Mount Ross Pounceys can be seen down to the left and it is an easy walk over the pastures to the start of the road. Matthew Pouncey was an early planter whose main claim to fame, according to Gosse, was for receiving 21 lashes in punishment for having called one of the Council a 'gallows building rogue'. He was a general troublemaker and ordered off the island in 1690 with his lands largely confiscated.

After about 150m you pass the small endemics reserve created by George Benjamin. The route back to White Gate can be made by following the road, but it is more interesting to turn left and cut across the playing field of St Paul's School, and so enter the back of St Paul's Cathedral cemetery. For the enthusiastic gravestone spotter St Helena's headstones offer a fine collection and the Cathedral cemetery is no exception. St Paul's was originally the new Country Church, built largely from prefabricated materials sent from England in 1850 to replace an earlier 17th-century church. In 1859 it was chosen by the inhabitants as the seat of the new Bishop, to become St Paul's Cathedral.

Oak Bank. (G. W. Melliss)

18 Casons Gate – Farm Buildings – Casons Gate

Elevation range: 700 – 550m
Length: 3km

This walk is circular and can be started at many points. For this description the start is taken from Casons Gate, where a car can easily be left. During the early 18th century Thomas Cason commanded the troop under seven successive Governors and drilled the soldiers better than those in India by using 'Colonel Bland's Method'; he owned a farm in the area named after him, but in 1711 sold it to the Government. The Casons Gate signal station became one of the most important tactical points on the island, with communication both to High Knoll and to Prosperous Bay via Long Range. For much of the year arum lilies, the emblem of St Helena, flower at Casons Gate; they are common in all the upland valleys, flowering from June onwards.

The initial section of the walk provides good views across the pastures of Lemon Valley Head to High Peak and Broad Bottom Farm (Walk 19). A wind pump can be seen below at Iron Pot. When working it is used to pump groundwater to Thompson's Hill. Iron Pot is named after the large whalers' trypot (formerly used for boiling whale blubber) around which a nearby thorn tree has grown. During the 19th century large numbers of whaling ships called at St Helena for rest and refreshment from hunting in the South Atlantic. The remains of an earlier wind pump can be seen below High Peak at Frenches Gut; this was blown down shortly after erection in the late 1970s, and an electric pump is now used.

After 200m the path narrows and passes Goldmine Gate; the origin of the name is obscure. At the base of the long rise to Thompson's Hill the track turns to the right and begins a gradual descent into Bevins Gut. The gut itself is delightfully lush and is

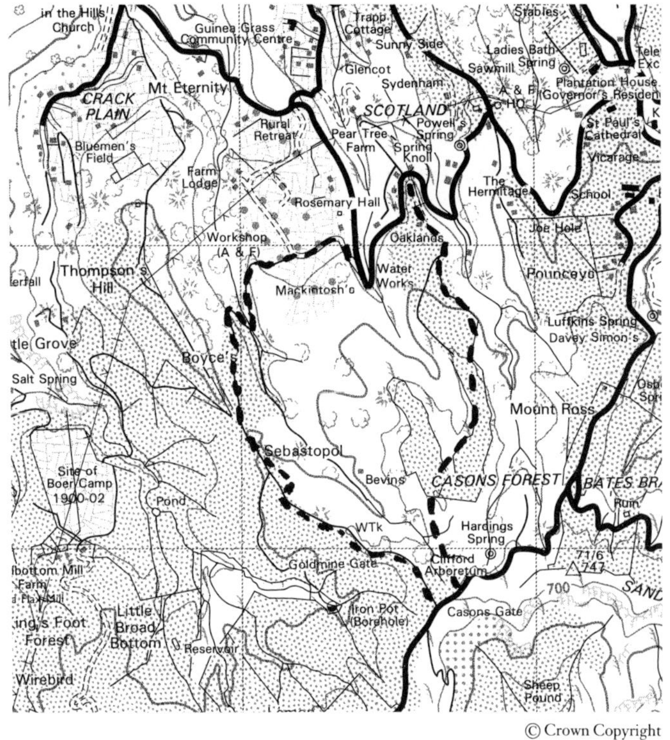

named after an early planter, Thomas Bevian, whose main claim to fame was for receiving 39 lashes for stealing a silver-headed cane in 1717.

The track becomes hard-surfaced as it approaches Farm Buildings. Feeding of livestock at Farm Buildings attracts flocks of Java sparrows. These attractive seedeaters, familiar as cagebirds, were introduced to St Helena from Indonesia in the early part of he 19th century. The Java sparrow has an almost hand-painted ppearance. It is quite unmistakable with pale blue-grey pperparts, black head and tail, white cheeks, lilac breast and large ed bill. Numbers seem to have fluctuated considerably since its ntroduction, but today the species is relatively common.

Above Farm Buildings the route joins the main road for a section, the route passes the green pastures of Mackintosh's and, on a sharp hairpin, the spring collection chambers in Spring Gut. Taking the route to Scotland, the road passes through a dark avenue of Cape yew; this South African tree produces very fine timber and is increasingly being planted to improve the island's timber resources. Around the next bend is the back entrance to Oaklands Hotel. Named after the now departed oaks that used to surround it, Oaklands has been restored recently, and is one of the island's more impressive houses dating from the 18th century. It is said to have been considered as a residence for Napoleon. Follow the road around to the main gate, and turn right up the drive. The drive is a public right of way, passing along the side of the house and up on to the pastures behind it.

There is no well defined path across the pastures, but by following the spine of the ridge you reach the fence marking the northern boundary of the Clifford Arboretum. Opened in 1977, the Arboretum is named after a former forestry officer, John Clifford. On the western side of the central ridge there are examples of forest trees introduced to the island, while the eastern side contains replanted endemics. Particularly interesting are the she-cabbage trees on the left of the track, just before exiting to the main road. These ancient plants are of the same family as daisies and are closely related to some of the relic fauna found on the high mountains of Africa.

Having reached the road it is just a few paces to the right to return to Casons Gate. It is worth crossing the road at this point to gain a splendid view of Sandy Bay Basin (see Walk 11).

'Mode of conveying hay.' (Graphic 1887)

19 Casons – Broad Bottom – Thompson's Hill – Casons

Elevation range: 800 – 550m
Length: 5km

This is another circular walk, with Casons Gate again making a convenient starting point (see Walk 18). The walk starts along the road with views across Lemon Valley Head. At the Frenches Gut corner it is possible to detour up High Peak (see Other Walks), or to continue on the lower road to the start of the track to Broad Bottom. The gut takes its name from an 18th-century troublemaker called Gunner John French.

Broad Bottom is one of the main centres of Solomons farming activity. The area is of interest through being the only substantial piece of land held continuously by one family from settlement (in the late 17th century) until transfer of the island to the Crown in 1834. The original owner was a Lieutenant Johnson, later the Governor murdered in the Jackson mutiny of 1693; the land passed by marriage to the Alexander family who held it until 1834. The buildings are the remains of one of the flax mills run by Deason Brothers (see Walk 21). During the Boers' captivity the cultivated area below the buildings was the site of a large tented prison camp holding over 1,000 prisoners. Friction developed at the first camp at Deadwood (Walk 5) between the 'Freestaters' and the 'Transvaalers'; in 1901 the camp at Broad Bottom was opened specifically for burghers of the Orange Free State.

A Boer prisoner of war provided one of the more amusing descriptions of St Helena's climate: 'There are two seasons (1) the rainy season, in which rain is the rule and sunshine the exception; (2) the dry season, which resembles the rainy one so much that the mistaking of one for the other has never yet been ascribed to ignorance'.

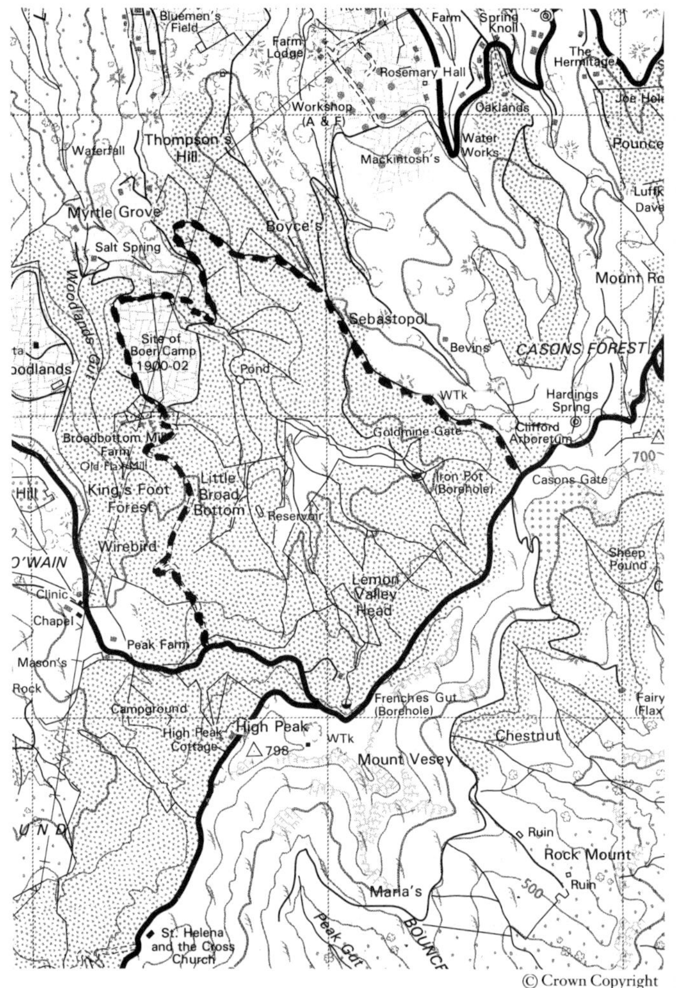

High Peak. (Burchell)

The pasturelands of Broad Bottom and Thompson's Hill hold considerable numbers of St Helena's smallest bird, the common waxbill (called the avadavat locally), which feeds on seeding grasses. This is a tiny brown finch with paler, greyish underparts suffused with pink, a relatively long black tail and a coral-red bill. Close views reveal the plumage to be finely barred. Waxbills are highly sociable and flocks may contain as many as 200 birds, though around 20 is more usual. Their call, a nasal, buzzing chirp, is very distinctive. Originally a native of southern African savannahs, the waxbill is another of St Helena's introduced species. So many were exported from the island as cagebirds during the 19th century that they became known in the pet trade as the St Helena waxbill.

Passing through Broad Bottom farmyard, the track runs around the top of the cultivated fields and down their western side before turning sharp right at the bottom and crossing a dry gut which is known as Broad Bottom Gut. Just up the gut from this point is an early attempt to construct a dam on St Helena made by Thornton, the then Solomons director, in the early 1970s. It holds water during wet periods but has never been used for anything other than supplying cattle. After crossing the gut the track forks. The left fork leads to Crack Plain and the right (to be followed for this walk) up Thompson's Hill to join the track on the ridge crest that leads back to Goldmine and Casons Gate. This section, which has already been described in Walk 18, takes about half an hour to complete.

20 Ball Alley – Blue Point – Old Lufkins

Elevation range: almost level
Length: 6km

This walk almost completes the route around the edge of the Sandy Bay 'crater', the eastern side of which is described in Walk 11. There are various starting points and different sections of the walk can be done at different times. It can also be linked with part of Walk 21 for a longer walk (in which case it is worth leaving a second car at the other end). In this description Ball Alley is taken as the start. In dry weather the new track leading from the Thompson's Wood – Botleys road is driveable, but in wet weather it is advisable to leave a car on the tarmac road.

The walk starts by crossing the pastures of the Churchyard – named from the scattering of boulders resembling gravestones in the area. Ball Alley is reached by the gate at the end of the pasture. It is an appropriate name for an area almost completely devoid of vegetation and lies in a gap between the Devil's Cap and Hooper's Ridge through which the trade winds are funelled. Much of the erosion is due to the wind in this area. The large dyke-like feature is the blasted remains of a wall built in the 1950s in an attempt to combat erosion.

From Ball Alley it is a 2km walk to Blue Point. The path passes through the garden of the romantically named Distant Cottage and then through a small area of flax before reaching the low ridge leading to Blue Point. (This is also the start of an alternative route to Lot's Wife Ponds via Lot's Wife but it is not recommended.) The views from the top of the ridge are spectacular, on the one side down the Devil's Hole and on the other along the coast to Sandy Bay Barn. The geology of the Sandy Bay Basin is mentioned in Walk 11. The phonolite intrusions of Lot, Lot's Wife and the Asses Ears can all be easily seen from this route.

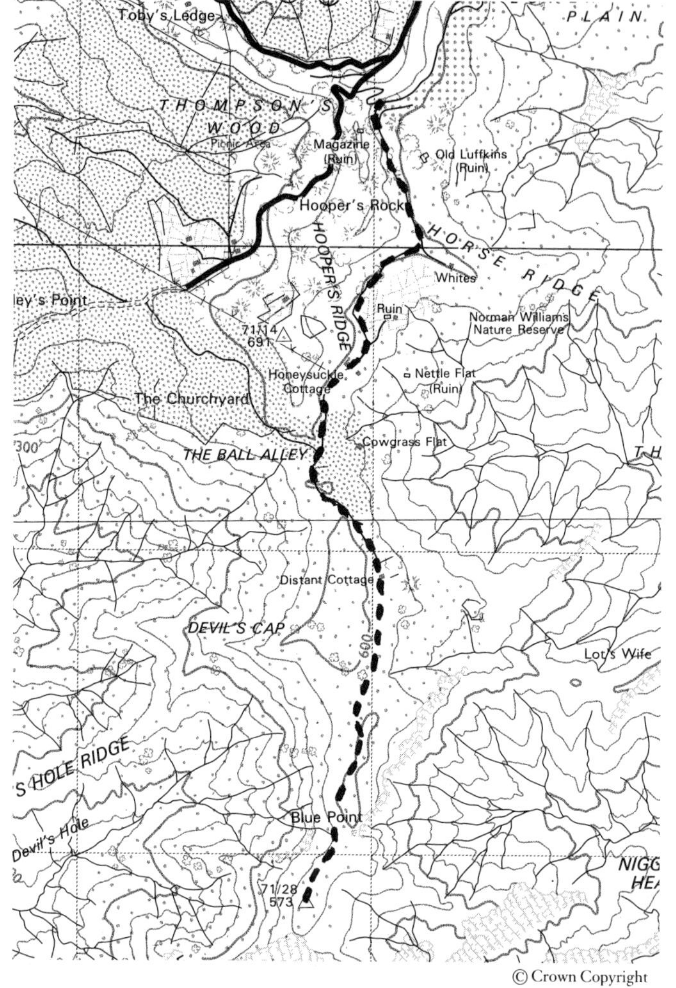

The walk to Blue Point is also of interest because of the flora. The St Helena plantain, growing up to one metre high, occurs around Distant Cottage as does the bushy scrubwood, with its daisy-like flowers most of the year. This is also the area in which George Benjamin discovered two examples of the St Helena ebony, clinging precariously to a cliff, in November 1980. This was a major find, as the ebony was nearly extinct by 1771 and was finally assumed to be extinct by about 1850. The plant has been successfully propagated since, and planted back out into the wild (see Walk 14).

Guano-covered Speery Island can be seen from Blue Point. This stack is a major breeding site for two of St Helena's rarer seabirds. The sooty tern, or wideawake, is a handsome bird, black above with gleaming white underparts. The face is also white with a black mask across the eyes. Although the sooty tern breeds in thousands on Ascension Island, the small St Helena population appears to be declining for unknown reasons.

Also breeding at Speery Island is the secretive Madeiran storm petrel. This 20-cm relative of the albatross is a dark bird with a prominent white rump patch. It flies in a distinctive zigzag manner close to the wave crests. Storm petrels nest in rock crevices and chicks are visited only during darkness. This species is rarely seen from the shore at St Helena, but individuals occasionally appear in James Bay, particularly at dusk.

Returning to Ball Alley, the route towards Fairyland is a track most of the way with the spectacular view of Sandy Bay a constant companion. The track initially passes the privately owned gardens at Nettle Flat before reaching the new Normal Williams Nature Reserve, created around the ruin of Horse Riding Hill House (also known as White's). An endemic reserve and a visitor centre are being established. Little is known about the building except that it was formerly owned by a Jamestown merchant called E. Hayward.

Leaving Horse Ridge the ruin of Old Lufkins soon comes into view. The delightfully situated house is owned by the Cairns-Wicks family. John Lufkin was responsible for the construction of both this house and the other one near Plantation also bearing his name. Lufkin was taken hostage by the Dennison mutineers of 1684; he was released, accused of conspiracy, but was later pardoned. On Hooper's Ridge above Old Lufkins there are the remains of an old picket house and magazine.

From Old Lufkins the path climbs through some flax and comes to a junction; the upward path continues back to the road at the northern end of Hooper's Ridge. By taking this route a circuit can be completed by walking down the road back to the point where the car was left. Alternatively the path towards Fairyland can be taken by turning right at the junction. This is described as Walk 21.

Old Lufkins. (Melitta Carter)

21 Old Lufkins – Fairyland – Bamboo Hedge

Elevation range: almost level
Length: 4.5km

It is a good idea on this walk to leave one car on the road above Old Lufkins (near the garage), and another at Bamboo Hedge. Starting from the path junction above Old Lufkins (Walk 20) the route goes down a short slope before levelling out. Immediately below lies Lower House Plain which contains the largest surviving area of gumwoods, an endemic tree that once covered much of the island. In the early years of settlement it was the major source of timber and firewood, although the tree is fairly small, reaching only about six metres with a very crooked frame. It is possible to reach the main wood by a scramble down from the path, but individual trees can be inspected more easily near the path just before reaching Peak Dale.

Peak Dale Farm lies in a beautiful setting immediately below High Peak, conjuring images of northern England as suggested by its name. John Des Fountain, the largest landowner during Napoleon's captivity, was a former owner. The farm is now one of the most inaccessible sites that is still inhabited.

From Peak Dale Farm the track crosses the gut and continues towards Fairyland. The next promontory is Rock Mount, the site of a new house; this property was owned by one of the island's most prominent farming families, the Bagleys, who arrived at St Helena with the refugees from the Great Fire of London. Continuing through an avenue of thorn trees, the track reaches Fairyland meadows and can be followed back up to the road at Casons or, by going through the gate, down to Fairyland flax mill.

Fairyland is named after the fairy terns that are common in this area (Walk 7). The mill, owned by the Thorpe family, replaced a fine country house, the property of Colonel Greentree, who created the Fairyland Estate in the 1850s. It is the only flax mill still in working order, although it is now seldom used. Flax is strictly New Zealand hemp – *Phormium tenax* – and quite distinct from linen flax. The plant was introduced to St Helena and first commercially worked in 1874. The industry lasted about 80 years, with two booms associated with the World Wars interspersed with long years of depression. At its peak in 1940 flax covered 1,350 hectares and its widespread planting resulted in the clearing of much pasture and endemic flora. Since the collapse of the industry in the 1960s, when artificial fibres replaced the hemp used in string, the flax areas have been steadily cleared and now cover only about 350 hectares. The cleared areas can be recognized by the strips of flax left while trees or grass are allowed to establish themselves in between. Although environmentally flax was undesirable, it was a major source of employment, and the main export for the first half of this century (in one year, early in the 1950s, the value of St Helena's exports exceeded its imports, the only occasion when this has been achieved). The other flax mills are in ruins, although some of the buildings have continued in use, such as at Broad Bottom, Woody Ridge and Bamboo Hedge.

From the grass yard in front of the mill there is an excellent view across the head of Sandy Bay Gut to the coffee grove. St Helena coffee won a prize at the Great Exhibition in 1851 but has suffered since from lack of continuity of supply. Recently, however, the entire annual crop has been purchased by a supplier based in Harrogate, who sells it as a specialist coffee.

The next stage of the walk is to Bamboo Hedge. It is necessary to walk down the grassy slope at the back of the mill to Sheep Pound in the bottom of the gut. After climbing the fence there is a short walk through some very dense flax before the path is reached. It is advisable to have someone to show the way at this point.

After crossing the gut the path passes through woodland; watch out for loquat trees with dark green shiny leaves and a yellow,

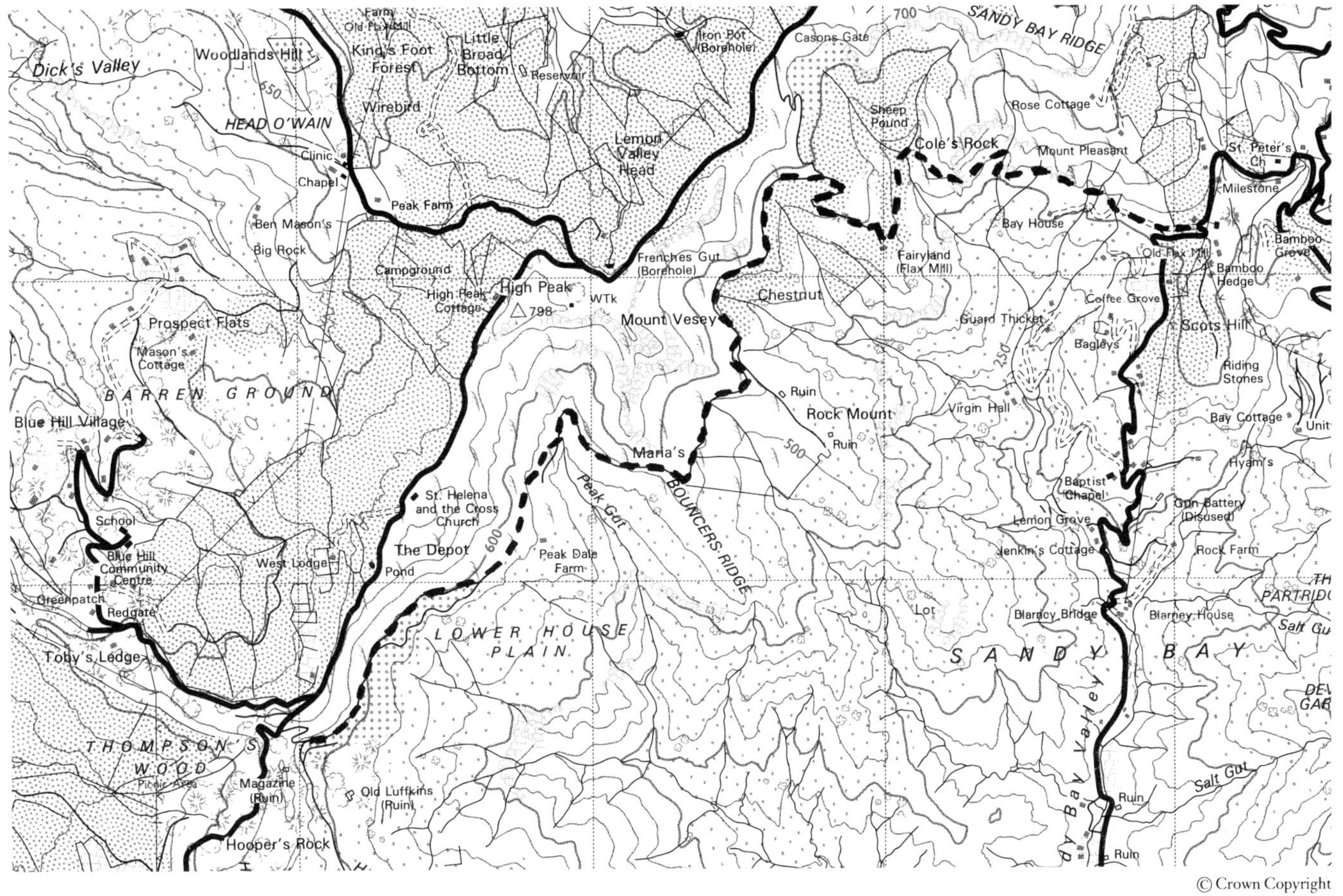
Dick's Valley
Woodlands Hill
HEAD O'WAIN
Clinic
Chapel
Ben Mason's
Big Rock
Prospect Flats
Mason's Cottage
BARREN GROUND
Blue Hill Village
School
Blue Hill Community Centre
Greenpatch
Redgate
Toby's Ledge
THOMPSON'S WOOD
Picnic Area
Magazine (Ruin)
Hooper's Rock
King's Foot Forest
Old Flax Mill
Little Broad Bottom
Reservoir
Wirebird
Peak Farm
Campground
High Peak Cottage
High Peak
798
WTk
Lemon Valley Head
Iron Pot (Borehole)
Frenches Gut (Borehole)
Mount Vesey
St. Helena and the Cross Church
The Depot
Pond
West Lodge
LOWER HOUSE PLAIN
Peak Gut
Peak Dale Farm
Maria's
BOUNCERS RIDGE
Old Luffkins (Ruin)
Casons Gate
SANDY BAY RIDGE
Sheep Pound
Cole's Rock
Fairyland (Flax Mill)
Chestnut
Ruin
Rock Mount
Rose Cottage
Mount Pleasant
Bay House
Guard Thicket
Virgin Hall
Baptist Chapel
Lemon Grove
Jenkin's Cottage
Lot
Blarney Bridge
SANDY BAY
Coffee Grove
Bagleys
St. Peter's Ch
Milestone
Old Flax Mill
Bamboo Grove
Bamboo Hedge
Scots Hill
Riding Stones
Bay Cottage
Hyam's
Gun Battery (Disused)
Rock Farm
Blarney House
Salt Gut
Sandy Bay Valley

Gumwood tree. (Burchell)

edible, plum-like fruit. The path emerges on to an open cliff top below Coles' Rock – which is best seen from Fairyland. In April 1721 a slave named Sultan murdered his master John Coles by 'throttling him with pieces of rope-yarn several times doubled and tying him by the throat to a root of a tree'. It seems that Sultan did not actually throw his master over the cliff, but was himself suspended in chains at the top of Ladder Hill for his crime.

From Coles' Rock until Bamboo Hedge the walk is through woodland and, although pleasant, there are no views. Bamboo Hedge is another centre of Solomons' farming activity and also an old flax mill. The house dates from the early 19th century. After rejoining the road at Bamboo Hedge there are various options, including a short walk down the hill to visit the coffee grove, or walking up the road to Sandy Bay school.

22 Halley's Mount – The Peaks – Teutonic

Elevation range: undulating 600 – 800m
Length: 2.5km

Fine weather is essential for a walk to the Peaks. A visit when the weather is bad is not only unpleasant but can also be dangerous, with visibility reduced to a few metres as the mists roll in. There are a number of alternative routes for exploring the area but some of the paths become overgrown very quickly, so access may be difficult in places. This and Walk 23 describe the main routes.

The walk starts at the sign that points to the path to Halley's Observatory on the road immediately above Hutts Gate. It is a short walk to the site of the observatory, the remains of which were rediscovered and excavated in 1970 (the site is a few metres off the path, to the left). Edmund Halley, after whom the comet is named, visited St Helena from February 1677 to March 1678. He needed a secure base which would allow him to tie in the stars of the southern hemisphere with those of the north. St Helena seemed ideal but he discovered only after he had established his observatory that he had picked one of the cloudiest spots on Earth. Nevertheless he was able to fulfil one of his main objectives, which was to determine the distance of the Earth from the sun by the transit of Mercury. He recommended that his work could be cross-checked by observing the transit of Venus, due 84 years later. Incredibly his recommendation was preserved and the astronomer Neville Maskelyne visited the island in 1761 to carry out the work. Although the site of his observatory was on the extension of Halley's Mount Ridge there is nothing left of it to see.

From Halley's Mount there is a superb view of Longwood and the south-east side of the island. Immediately below lies St Matthew's Church (built in 1862), the charming Hutts Gate store and, on the hill opposite, the site of St Helena's first full

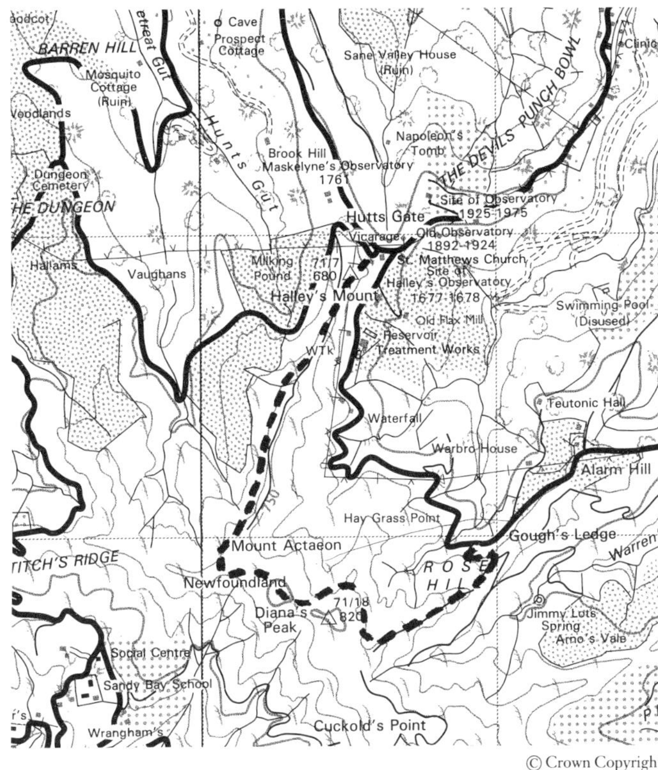

Meteorological Station, established in 1892. There is also a good view of the Hutts Gate treatment works that collects spring water from the Peaks for distribution to Longwood.

The path continues along the back of the ridge through the flax and up towards the Peaks with Grapevine Gut on the right. It joins the Cabbage Tree Road and for a short section follows the same

'Halleys Mount and Hutts Gate from Woody Ridge.' (Graphic 1880)

course as Walk 23. If the Peaks are to be visited that description should be consulted.

To continue on this walk follow the path around the north-eastern side of the Peaks, skirting under the heights of Diana's Peak. The extreme steepness of the ridges can be appreciated from this route, while elsewhere the density of the vegetation largely obscures the near vertical hill sides. If you know where to look you can see (with binoculars) the last remaining wild specimen of the St Helena olive, discovered by George Benjamin in August 1977, by looking back to the upper slopes of Mt Actaeon. The St Helena olive is quite distinct from the wild olive, which is a tree of the middle levels. Neither is any relation of the true olive, but the wild olive does have olive-like fruit – albeit white.

During wet periods this path can be very muddy as several springs issue in its general vicinity. Eventually the route comes out on pasture land above Teutonic Hall and it is a short walk down the hill to the road. The strikingly European appearance of St Helena's pastures is emphasized by the presence of pheasants. The male, with its long tail and green, red and coppery colouring, is unmistakable. Females are greyish-brown. The pheasant was another very early introduction by the Portuguese. Although intensively hunted during the short open season, a healthy population remains today. Their tendency to remain in thick cover limits the chance of their being seen by the casual visitor but the edges of high pastures fringed with flax or other dense vegetation provide the best opportunities, particularly in early morning and at dusk.

The walk back to Hutts Gate by the road provides excellent views of both the Peaks above and the head of Fisher's Valley below. Most of the springs that cross the road have been picked up by the pipeline which runs parallel to the road.

23 Cabbage Tree Road – The Peaks – Wranghams

Elevation range: 500 – 800m
Length: 2.5km

On this walk it is advisable to leave a car at either end. The start is signposted 'Cabbage Tree Road' and follows a grassy track through the flax. This track was part of Sir Hudson Lowe's 'New Military Road' and with Walk 22 follows its line until it emerges near Teutonic Hall; from here the road was continued to Woody Ridge for the benefit of Napoleon's excursions.

Thorn trees and the flower-heads of flax along the roads leading to the Peaks provide song-posts for the most colourful of St Helena's introduced songbirds. The male Madagascar fody (known on the island as the cardinal or robin) is unmistakable during the breeding season when head and breast are intense scarlet. After breeding the plumage of the male resembles that of females, which is buff-brown without any distinctive markings. Like that of most brilliantly coloured birds, the fody's song is unremarkable, consisting of a rapid series of buzzy chirps. Fodies are seedeaters related to the weaver birds of Africa and their nest is a flimsy basketwork of grass and fibres. Fodies are usually sociable and flocks of up to 200 may be encountered feeding on areas of short grass such as Francis Plain and Longwood Golf Course (Walks 16, 25).

After a few twists the top of the ridge is reached and there are spectacular views of Sandy Bay and down to Wranghams, the destination for this walk which is almost vertically below. Among many sites that can be pointed out from here, one of the more interesting is the appropriately named Mount Pleasant. This house was the destination of Napoleon's last visit from Longwood on 4 October 1820. He took tea on Sir William Doveton's lawn; at an earlier dinner with the Emperor, Doveton had caused a stir by keeping his hat on throughout, but this clearly had not unduly upset Napoleon. In the opposite direction the green pastures of James Valley head provide an astonishing contrast to the barren landscape on the southern side of the island.

Shortly after the view point the first tree ferns appear. These are the most distinctive of St Helena's endemic flora, having a 2-3 metre high trunk and grow in groups to form a thicket. Also on the Peaks are examples of the black cabbage tree, he- and she-cabbage trees, whitewood, the dogwood, jellico, the St Helena lobelia, large and small bellflowers and the single surviving St Helena olive. The endemics, and particularly the cabbage trees, on the Peaks have suffered clearance not only because of flax but also because of an experiment to cultivate cinchona. The bark of cinchona is used to make quinine and attempts to grow it on St Helena between 1868-70 were encouraged by the eminent Director of Kew Gardens, Sir Joseph Hooker. While it is unlikely that it would ever have been an economic success in such difficult terrain, the plants liked the environment and their successors are still common on Mt Actaeon. The experiment, like so many on the island, was terminated by the succeeding Governor, but the optimistic name Newfoundland still applies to the southern side of the Peaks. It is ironic that it should have been Hooker who promoted this unwitting destruction of endemics for, following his visits with the Ross Antarctic Expedition, he had great influence on J. C. Melliss and much to do with bringing the uniqueness of St Helena's flora to international attention.

Continuing up the Cabbage Tree Road, the route passes the junction with the path (to the left) to Halley's Mount (Walk 22). Next a V junction is reached. The right fork passes to the south side of the Peaks and is the start of the route to Wranghams. An old nine-pounder cannon lies next to the track and is thought to have been part of an alarm system probably dating from

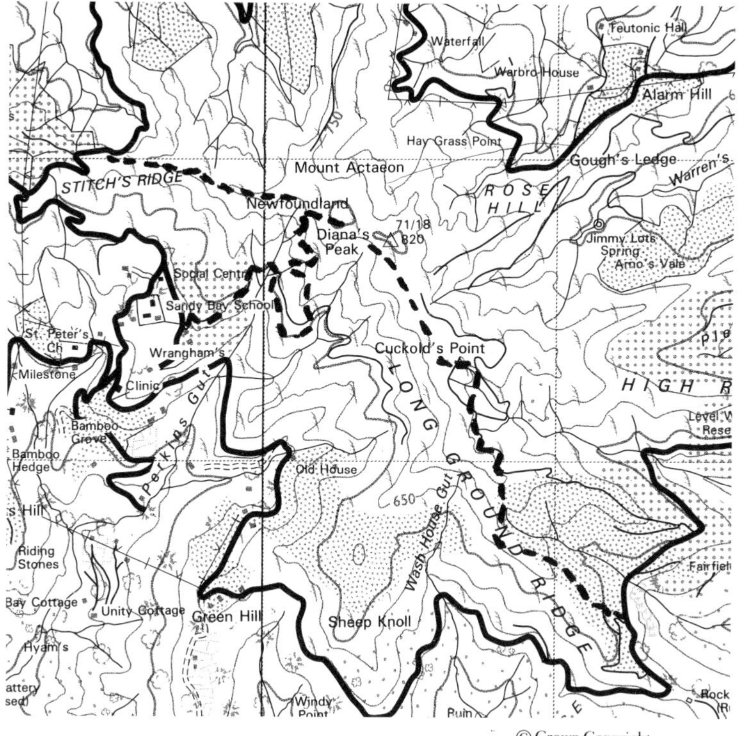

Napoleonic times. Before heading down, a visit to the summit of the Peaks should not be missed.

To do this continue a short distance on the path on the north side of the Peaks; there is a rather overgrown path to the right that climbs by steps to the top of Mt Actaeon. The top is marked by a weatherbeaten Norfolk Island pine, as is the other end of the ridge, Cuckhold's Point. The highest point, Diana's Peak, is treeless and in the middle. The walk along the central ridge is rewarding for the views of both sides of the island, while vegetation conceals the steepness of the knife-edge ridge. On Diana's Peak there is a rubber stamp to allow cards to be franked to commemmorate a visit.

The names of the three peaks are the subject of one of St Helena's more extraordinary and long-running controversies. The case has been argued for the sequence of names to run from the south Diana, Actaeon, Cuckhold's or Actaeon, Diana, Cuckhold's. The sequence used in this description is that used on the current maps – Cuckhold's, Diana, Actaeon – but as to which is 'correct' there will probably never be agreement.

Returning to the junction for Wranghams the walk down is overgrown in places but fairly straightforward. The path emerges on a new forestry track which can be followed down to the 18th-century home of a Mr and Mrs Wrangham.

24 Teutonic – Pleasant Valley – Silver Hill

Elevation range: 500 – 600m
Length: 3km

This walk starts at the end point of Walk 22 and near the start of the drive to Teutonic Hall. Teutonic Hall used to be known as Mason's after an earlier owner named Miss Polly Mason; it is said that she used to signal to Napoleon at Longwood from her back window. He could be clearly seen from Mason's when walking in Longwood garden. The name was changed from Mason's to Teutonic in 1822 by G. W. Janisch, the father of St Helena's only island-born Governor, Hudson Ralph Janisch. Immediately below Teutonic lies the ruin of Walbro Hall which was granted to the slave Black Oliver for his assistance with the English landing at Prosperous Bay in 1673 (see Walk 7).

From the road follow the winding track up past the tank on the top of the ridge at Gough's Ledge. Some green and red marker posts indicate the route. From here there is a steady descent through the flax, but watch out for the marker posts to keep on the correct route.

At the bottom of the hill after several twists and turns the path crosses Warrens Gut. Here it is best to continue straight up the hill on the other side of the gut, although a left turn along the gut ultimately ends at the same point as the upper route. Jimmy Lot's spring lies a few metres upstream from this point and is used as a source of water for Woody Ridge and Tobacco Plain.

Continuing up the sharp rise on the other side of the gut, the walk opens out on to the pastures of Arno's Vale. Apart from a small potato field, this is part of Solomons' grazing lands. The origins of the name are obscure but during Napoleon's captivity there was a substantial house at Arno's Vale which was used as a convalescent home, notably by Ensign George Heathcote who for

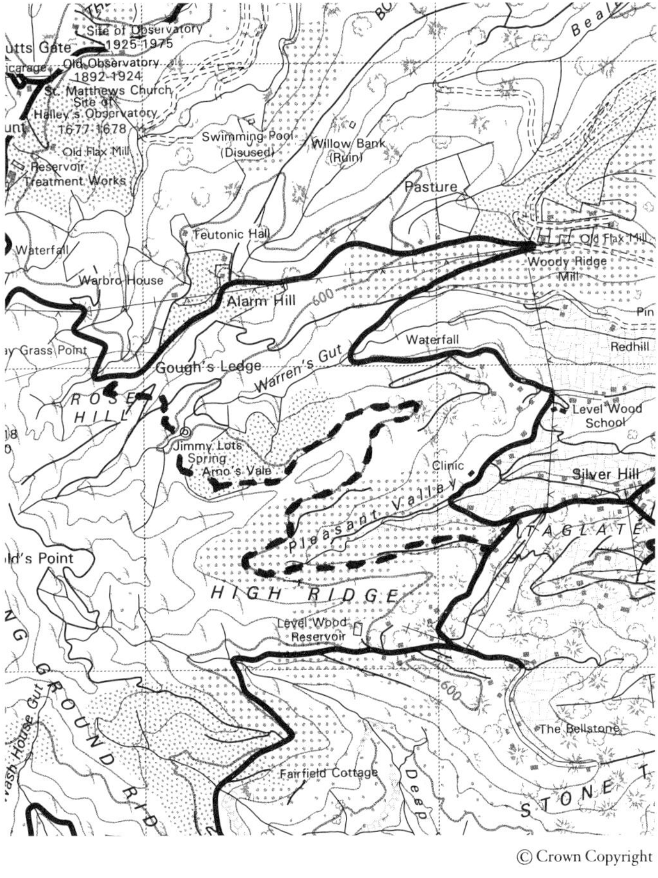

a time was of romantic interest to Napoleon's friend Betsy Balcombe. Later the house was owned for a short time by G.W. Janisch, but it has now almost disappeared.

The walk continues down the hill to the lower pastures across which there is a well defined track; but there may be a bull in this field, so beware! Cross the fence at the end of the field and the path becomes a track with almost level going through open woodland. This is the old route around the Peaks to Levelwood and beyond and it was in the vicinity of Arno's Vale that Napoleon gave Poppleton the slip on his flight to Rock Rose (see Walk 10).

From now on the path stays in woodland almost the whole way to Silver Hill, although it emerges at one point to give a view across Levelwood. Towards the end the woodland changes from mixed species to the eucalyptus plantations of Pleasant Valley; these were established during the 1970s on cleared flax land. Cape gooseberries, locally known as bilberries, grow in abundance along the side of the path throughout much of the year and are good for cooking and making jam (as well as eating immediately).

The route eventually emerges just above Silver Hill bar which is also the start of Walk 8 to Sharks Valley.

25 Longwood Gate – Fisher's Valley – Longwood Gate

Elevation range: 350 – 520m
Length: 7km

This is a circular walk that is well suited for a start at Piccolo Hill. The route approximates to one that was followed by Napoleon several times during his first few months at Longwood.

Piccolo Hill was built during the 1960s to house the staff of the Diplomatic Wireless Service. With the aid of an aerial complex on Prosperous Bay Plain the DWS, whose call sign was Piccolo, was able to monitor most West African radio communications until satellites and more powerful transmitters made their services redundant.

From Piccolo follow the road past the golf course down to Bottom Woods. A small area of the golf course is on the left-hand side of the road; at the far side of this is probably the finest single gumwood tree on the island, with Flagstaff as a fine backdrop. The bent trees on the course itself demonstrate the power and constancy of the south-east trade winds. During dry periods when the grass is brown, patches of green occur on the downwind side of the trees due to mist interception by the foliage.

After the golf course the road bends through the multicoloured cottages of Bottom Woods and past the paddocks before making a sharp right turn towards the Government garage at Bradleys. At this point a right fork on to a dirt track is the route for Fisher's Valley. A detour may be made past the rubbish dump, across the carpet of mesembryanthemum to Horse Point where, in the late 1960s, a Belgian expedition made the last sighting of the St Helena earwig, which is now presumed extinct. On the way back there is a fenced area of recent endemic planting, mainly of scrubwood and gumwood; there is also a particularly fine and large scrubwood

Horse Point. (Burchell)

specimen that is about eight metres wide but only one metre high.

The track continues down to Fisher's Valley across one of the most eroded areas of the island. The soils are rich in sodium, which facilitates their erosion by water (see Walk 8) and wind. The colours are spectacular and have been romanticized by such names as the Artist's Palette; the colours even encouraged Burchell in 1808 to send samples for analysis in England, in the hope of discovering precious minerals. However, in reality the area is an example of the worst ravages of goat and man, and is beyond hope of reclamation.

The track reaches the bottom of Fisher's Valley at Cook's Bridge (Walk 7). From here turn right, following the track up the right side of the valley. The lush pastures provide a stark contrast to the eroded and bare hummocks along the valley side. Fisher's Valley is unique among St Helena valleys in being relatively flat-bottomed and shallow-sided; the reason for this is the erodible

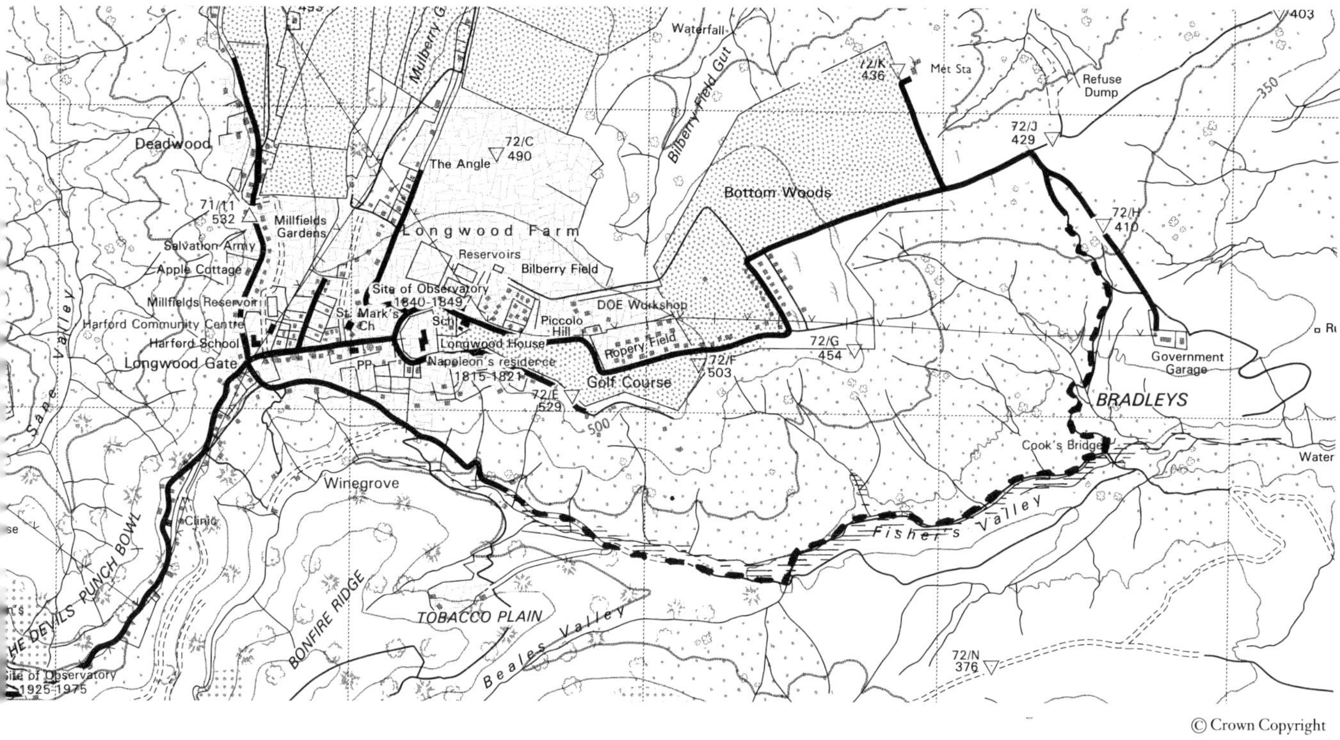

nature of the soils that become quickly unstable and washed away on steeper slopes.

The marshy area around Cook's Bridge is a good place for seeing moorhens. Moorhens are quite common in wet valleys throughout St Helena, but are secretive and wary. They probably became established naturally after the discovery of the island, filling the niche left by the extinction of the rails. The moorhen is black with white patches on the flanks and under the tail. It has bright yellow-green legs and a yellow-tipped red bill. The pools and puddles at Cook's Bridge also attract wirebirds (see Walk 5). The birds tolerate vehicles, and these can be used as hides from which to obtain photographs. Mid-afternoon visits usually produce most wirebirds.

After about 1.5km the track crosses to the south side of the valley and there is a curious boggy fenced oval by the side of the track. On the opposite hill side the scars bear witness to an attempt to build a major dam in the 1950s to supply an irrigation scheme on Prosperous Bay Plain. The oval is the remains of an attempt to excavate a trench (with picks and shovels) into solid rock to provide a base for the dam. The site proved too wet and most of the money for the project was used just constructing the perimeter fence that is still in evidence.

The track comes to a junction from where a detour can be made (to the left) to see the private vegetable gardens of Tobacco Plain. The route to Longwood follows the valley for a few hundred metres before it once again becomes tarmacked and there is a long haul back up to Longwood Gate. The gate was built in the early 18th century and later became Dolly's Chop House, serving tourists visiting Longwood.

From here it is a short walk through the avenue of cedars to Piccolo. Along the way of course is Longwood House, but a less well known building is St Mark's Church, which lies just behind Solomons Supermarket. This building was erected in 1840 as the Longwood Observatory for magnetic observations – part of a network of observatories around the British Empire. The equipment was brought to the island in the ships *Erebus* and *Terror* (subsequently lost with Franklin's expedition to the North-West Passage) under James Clark Ross on his way to Antarctica. The observatory was run by Lieutenant J. H. Lefroy, later Governor of Bermuda (1870-77) and Tasmania (1880-81).

Longwood Old House. (G. W. Melliss)

Marshall Bertrand's Cottage. (G. W. Melliss)

26 Other Walks and Points of Interest

In the book we have described most of St Helena's well known walks. Most take at least an afternoon to complete, and a full day should be set aside for some. But there are a large number of other routes, both short and long, that should not be missed if there is time available. There are also many places of either historical interest or natural beauty (or even just for a picnic) that do not involve specific walks. Some of the best are as follows:

(A) ON THE COAST

Deep Valley (Walk 9) is a walk that could be attempted by the more intrepid walker. Its inaccessibility has meant that it was never fortified.

A few hundred metres above Prosperous Plain is an old **signal station** (see Walk 7), near **King and Queen Rocks**. The station was the site of a murder in 1905 when the brothers Richard and Lewis Crowie shot and killed Signalman Gunnell for his money. Their subsequent execution in the Old Power House in Jamestown was the last on the island. The executioner's rope can still be seen upon application to the Chief of Police.

The walk to **Dry Gut** starts at the old flax mill at Woody Ridge and continues via Bencoolen (named after the town in Sumatra which was an important trading centre for the East India Company). The route gives more views of the eroded south-east side of the island. There is a good, if not very encouraging, view from the top of Bencoolen down the proposed airstrip on Prosperous Bay Plain.

From Sandy Bay beach a walk up **Broad Gut** provides good views of Lot's Wife and a close up of the generally barren nature of the Sandy Bay basin. However, there is no easy way out of the head of the valley so it is simplest to return to the beach at the end of the walk.

A walk on **Man and Horse Pastures** is very pleasant during good weather. The walk can be started at Botleys; the track runs up through the sheep pastures. There are views of Speery Island and this is the best place to watch trophy birds (see Walk 1). More than 50 birds can often be seen soaring on the updraught along the 600m precipice – an unforgettable sight. At South-West Point there is the ruin of a 19th-century signal station that was also used during World War 1. At the bottom of the neighbouring Water Gut is a sheep pound.

The walk along **Goat Pound Ridge** starts at Cleughs Plain with precipitous drops to Friar's Valley on one side and Youngs Valley on the other. There are good views along the coast from the three ruined batteries on the end of the ridge.

The beach opposite **Egg Island** is a good destination for a day out by boat. The island lies at the mouth of Old Woman's Valley and is connected to the mainland by a narrow spit of rocks known as a tombolo; this is now largely submerged, but within recorded history was above sea level. Egg Island was, and still is, the nesting ground for two species of dark terns known as noddies. It can be difficult for the inexperienced observer to separate the species, close views being required. The larger species is the brown noddy, which is wholly chocolate-brown except for a greyish-white cap extending from forehead to crown. The wings have a two-tone appearance, being darker at the tip and trailing edge. The black noddy is much darker brown, black at a distance, but has a more extensive pure white cap and a longer and finer bill. Black noddies build bracket nests of seaweed and guano on sheer cliff faces. A boat trip to Egg Island between October and March will provide the best views of both species.

In the early years of the colony sea-bird eggs were an important food source; guano was also collected. In the 1840s there was a brief guano-based 'boom' in the South Atlantic, centred around islands off south-west Africa, but also affecting St Helena and Ascension. In St James' Church there is a tablet commemorating George Singer 'who was accidentally precipitated from off Egg Island while faithfully serving his employers' – he probably fell while collecting guano. In the records a John Lavery's body was found in the belly of a shark that was caught by some fishermen; he was thought to have been surprised while he slept on Egg Island; this is the only recorded fatality due to sharks in St Helena's coastal waters. Cockburn's Battery, named after the Admiral who accompanied Napoleon on board HMS *Northumberland*, has a well preserved cannon on top of the island and can be reached with some difficulty. The battery also has a furnace for heating shot – the only one now left on St Helena.

(B) INLAND, INCLUDING PICNIC SPOTS

There are two officially designated picnic spots at **Thompson's Wood** (see Walk 14) and **Horse Pasture**. **Half Moon**, just below Head O'Wain clinic is another nice picnic spot, although it is privately owned by the Cairns-Wicks family (the name Head O'Wain probably comes from Head of Vein, on account of it being at the end of a stratum of rock). **Willowbank** at the head of Fisher's Valley is green and lush throughout the year and in dry weather it is possible to drive down to it. There is an old swimming pool here built by Tony Thornton. Some way below the pool is the site of a recent unsuccessful attempt to build a dam, but water is abstracted from boreholes in the area and pumped up to Hutts Gate. During Napoleon's captivity Willowbank was an important estate owned by John Legg and Napoleon visited the farm to discuss agriculture with the owner. Hutts Gate was the gate to the estate. Just before **Rock Rose** (coming from Levelwood), there are the ruins of an old flax mill. The flat area offers a good spot for a picnic, with excellent views.

Climbing **High Hill** is a pleasant way to spend half a day. High Hill is a phonolite intrusion – the largest on the island – and is therefore of the same structure as Lot and Lot's Wife. It is possible to park at the base of the Hill and the path up is easily negotiated through thin pine forest. The path starts close to the car park, and leads off round to the right side of the Hill. Having reached the summit there is then a short walk along the crest of the ridge, from which vertiginous drops and spectacular views compete for attention. The ruins of an old look-out post overlook Ebony Plain.

A climb up **High Peak** should not be omitted from a visit to St Helena. It is a short sharp climb to one of the highest points on the island. It can be undertaken on its own, or as part of another walk, such as Walk 19. The ascent starts from the road at Frenches Gut. Half-way up there is a large concrete water tank that collects the groundwater pumped from Frenches Gut and feeds it by gravity to the western side of the island. By following the fence running behind the tank, a stile is reached. Across this lies the richest concentration of endemic flora off Diana's Peak. There are black cabbage trees whose daisy-like flowers appear in the spring, he- (but not she-) cabbage trees, a smaller cabbage tree known as whitewood, dogwood (a different natural order from the island's other endemics), tree ferns, St Helena lobelia and the creeping plants known as small and large bellflowers. The area is of considerable international significance and should be treated accordingly. Geologically High Peak is of no special interest, being a slightly more resistant section of the main volcanic shield.

'Napoleon's tomb.' (Graphic 1890)

From the stile it is a short climb to the summit, which is marked by Norfolk Island pines. The view from the top is one of the best on St Helena. There is about a 345° view of the ocean, blocked only by Diana's Peak. To the north lie the lush pastures of Lemon Valley and to the south the barren wastes of Sandy Bay. High Peak is frequently shrouded in mist, which can close in and reduce visibility to a few metres within minutes. This is the damp misty environment that is favoured by so many of the endemic flora. A descent can be made down the west side of High Peak; crossing the road and the pastures immediately below, the walker emerges at the start of the track to Broad Bottom.

A walk up to the **Heart Shape Waterfall** can be enjoyable, particularly when water is flowing over it. Take the Constitution Hill road out of Jamestown and turn off to the right towards Drummonds Point (before going up to the Briars). After 200-300m a break in the wall marks the start of the path to the waterfall, descending sharply at first to cross some of the intakes for the Jamestown water supply. It was in this general area (for there is no precise record) that Governor Blackmore slipped from his horse and fell to his death in 1691, from a path that no longer exists. The path to the waterfall is little more than a scramble up the valley over rocks and undergrowth, but the effort is well worthwhile. It is possible to walk behind the waterfall.

Diana's Peak Ring Road. The problem with driving on St Helena is that many of the roads have flax hedges running along them that hide the view from a car. Walking is a different matter and keeping to the tarmac offers some nice routes; Diana's Peak Ring Road is about 18km long and provides good views of all sides of the island. It is hard work to complete but can be shortened by, for example, taking a cut across the Peaks. Along the way Green Hill provides a good picnic spot with fine views across Sandy Bay basin.

A visit to **Napoleon's Tomb** should not be missed. It is possible to approach by the old route from near Hutts Gate, but the signposted route is much the easiest. It was cut especially for the funeral cortège. The famous willows that used to surround the tomb have now gone and Norfolk Island pines with their distinctive cones are predominant. Napoleon visited the site once and chose it for his burial. He had a Chinese servant bring him water daily from the spring to have with his wine. The tomb has no inscription, as Hudson Lowe would only permit the name 'Napoleon Buonaparte' to be used, which was unacceptable to the French. The body was disinterred in 1840, 25 years to the day after the Emperor arrived on St Helena, and now lies in Les Invalides by the River Seine in Paris.

By coincidence Napoleon was buried on St Helena at the head of the **Sane Valley** (although the latter is named after the landowner prior to Napoleon's time). A walk through the upper end of Sane Valley starts by taking the track opposite the green water tank on the Devil's Punch Bowl Road between Hutts Gate and Longwood; there is not a clearly defined path but the route lies through a pine wood out on to the Sane Valley pastures, past Fox's Folly where there is a man-made cave (possibly made by Chinese labourers) and ending at Alarm Cottage.

There is a very pleasant walk through **Plantation Forest**. The route starts at White Gate and continues around the back of Plantation House before joining a track at Ladies Bath Spring (so named from a wash-house formerly used by the ladies of Government House). There is a large clump of giant bamboo nearby. The track winds through the most diverse forest on the island and emerges at the Scotland sawmill and Department of Agriculture offices.

High Knoll fort offers excellent views and is a good orientation

'Plantation House.' (Graphic 1890)

spot. A fort has existed on the site since 1790 but the present structure is relatively modern, being built by the Royal Engineers between 1874 and 1894. Probably its most vital duty was to serve for incarcerating the more dangerous of the Boer prisoners. Currently it is used as an intermittent animal quarantine centre and as the Geoceiver base operated by the US Government for tracking satellites.

A stroll around the baptist cemetery at **Knollcombes** is very pleasant. Here is the memorial to the only island-born governor,

Hudson Janisch, and also the stepped graves of the Boer prisoners who died during a typhoid epidemic. The nearby house was owned by the commander of the Garrison in 1823 – a brigadier general who had the improbable surname Pine Coffin.

There is a good camping/picnic spot at **West Lodge**. Walk from Blue Hill school around the bowl-shaped head of the valley (there is a path around the bowl) and you emerge near West Lodge and St Helena and the Cross Church. There are also numerous paths through the forest in the Blue Hill area.

'We are at Napoleon's tomb, weary and thirsty.' (Graphic 1886)

'And our festivity comes to an end.' (Graphic 1886)

Ladies garden, Plantation House. (Burchell)

References and Recommended Reading

The main sources of information used to write this guide are held by the public library in Jamestown or the archives, which are located in the Castle. Some of the books can be bought either locally or on the ship. Maps of St Helena are available in the Post Office. Principal sources used were as follows:

Brooks, Mabel. *St Helena Story* (1960)

Cross, A. *St Helena* (1980)

Denholm, K. *St Helena, South Atlantic Fortress.* Fortress Magazine (1990)

Edwards, A. *Fish and Fisheries of St Helena Island* (1990)

Gosse, Philip. *St Helena 1502-1938* (1938, reprinted 1990)

Holland, M. (ed). *The Endemic Flora of St Helena* (SHG 1986)

Jackson, E.L. *St Helena: The Historic Island* (1903)

Janisch, Hudson. *Extracts from the St Helena Records* (reprinted by W.A.Thorpe 1981)

Kitching, G.C. 'A Handbook and Gazetteer of the Island of St Helena' including a Short History of the Island under the Crown 1834-1902 (typewritten manuscript (1937), original held in Plantation House library)

Norwood Young. *Napoleon in Exile at St Helena* (1915)

St Helena Magazine. Extracts from issues 1920-51 held by the Jamestown archives

Weaver, Barry. *A Guide to the Geology of St Helena* (1990)

Williams, R.O. *Plants of St Helena* (1977) (report reproduced by Agriculture & Natural Resources Department 1988)

Several of the illustrations used in this book are by William John Burchell who was resident on St Helena 1805-10 as schoolmaster and acting botanist. This was the early stage of what proved to be a distinguished African botanical career. His collection of botanical and scenic views are held by the Royal Botanic Gardens, Kew.

Illustrations have also been taken from *Views of St Helena – Illustrative of its Scenery and Historical Associations from Photographs* by G.W.Mellis 1857. Mellis was surveyor general and the father of J.C.Mellis who produced the definitive *St Helena* in 1875.

Index

Figures refer to walk number; In = Introduction;
J = Jamestown walk

Places

Airstrip 7
Alarm Cottage 26
Arno's Vale 24
Artificial Reef 1
Ascension 5
Asses Ears 20

Bagleys 21
Ball Alley 20
Bamboo Hedge 12a, 21
Banks Battery In, 4
Banks Platform 4
Banks Ridge 3
Banks Valley 4
Barn, the 5, 11
Barnes Road 16
Bates Branch 17
Bay Point 7
Beach Hill 12a
Bellstone, the 9
Bencoolen 26
Bevins Gut 18
Bilberry Gut 6
Billy Birch Cliff 10, 11
Bishops Bridge 17
Black Bridge 16
Black Point 6
Blue Point 20
Botleys 13, 20
Bottom Woods 6, 25
– Weather Station 6
Boxwood Hill 9
Bradleys 7, 25
Breakneck Valley 1
Briars, the 16
Briars Gut 16
Broad Bottom 18, 19, 21
Broad Bottom Gut 19
Broad Gut 12, 12a, 26
Broadway House J
Bulk Fuel Installation 3, 4
Buttermilk Point 4

Cabbage Tree Road 22, 23
Canister J
Cape Town 15
Casons Gate 18, 19, 21
Castle J
Cathedral 17
Cavalho Hole 4
Country School 17
Cowpath 2
Chubbs Rock 2
Chimney, the 12
Churchyard, the 14, 20
Cleughs Plain 26
Clifford Arboretum 18
Coles' Rock 21
Consulate Hotel J, 2
Cook's Bridge 7, 25
Cornelian mine 6
Cox's Battery 6
Crack Plain 15, 19
Cuckhold's Point 23

Deadwood In, 3, 5, 19
Deep Valley 9, 26
Devil's Cap 20
Devil's Hole 20
Devil's Punch Bowl 26
Diana's Peak 22, 23, 26
Diana's Peak Ring Road 26
Distant Cottage 20
Dolly's Chop House 25
Donkey Plain 7
Drummonds Point 16, 26
Dry Gut 7, 26

Eagle's Eyrie 13
Ebony Plain 13, 26
Egg Island 26
Elephant Rock 8

Fairyland 20, 21
Farm Buildings 18
Field Road 2
Fisher's Valley 7, 22, 25
Flagstaff 4, 5, 6
Fox's Folly 26
Francis Plain 3, 16, 23
Francis Plain House 16
Frenches Gut 19
Friar's Rock 15
Friar's Ridge 15
Friar's Valley 26

Goat Pound Ridge 15, 26
Goldmine Gate 18, 19
Golf course 23, 25
Gough's Ledge 24
Government Garage J
Grand Parade J
Grapevine Gut 22
Great Wood 6
Great Stone Top 8, 9
Green Hill 10, 11, 26
Gregory's Battery 6

Half Tree Hollow 1, 2
Half Moon (pasture) 26
Half Moon Battery (Banks) 4
Half Moon Battery (Lemon Valley) 15
Halley's Mount 22, 23
Hancock Hole 8
Haystack, the 5
Head o'Wain 26
Heart Shape Waterfall 16, 26
High Hill 14, 26
High Knoll 2, 3, 18, 26
High Peak 18, 19, 21, 36
Holdfast Tom 7
Hooper's Ridge 14, 20
Horse Pasture 26
Horse Point 25
Horse Ridge Hill House 20
Horse's Head 12a
Hospital, the 2
Hutts Gate 22, 26

Iron Pot 18

Jacob's Ladder 2
James Bay 20, J
Jamestown In, 1, 2, 3, 4, 7, 15, 16, 26

James Valley 2
– Old Power House 7
Jimmy Lot's Spring 24
Jubilee Coldstore J

King and Queen Rocks 26
King William's Fort 4
Knollcombes 26
Knotty Ridge 5, 6

Ladder Hill J, 2
Ladies Bath Spring 26
Lemon Tree Gut 16
Lemon Valley 15, 18, 19
Levelwood 8, 9, 23, 24
Library J
Little Stone Top 9
Long Ground Ridge 23
Longwood 5, 22, 24, 25, 26
Longwood Farm 6
Longwood Gate 25
Longwood House 25
Longwood Observatory 25
Lot and Lot's Wife 9, 20, 26

Malabar Store J
Maldivia 2
Main Street J
Man and Horse 13, 26
Manati Bay 13
Market, public J
Mason's 24
Middle Point (Longwood) 6
Middle Point Battery 4
Mt Actaeon 22, 23
Mt Pleasant 23
Mulberry Gut 6
Mundens Battery In, 2

Newfoundland 23
Netley Gut 6
Nettle Flat 20
Norman Williams Nature Reserve 20

Oakbank 17
Oaklands 18
Old Lufkins 20, 21
Old Woman's Valley 15, 26
Osborne's 17

Peak Dale 21
Peak Hill 16
Peaks, the 22, 23, 26
Piccolo Hill 25
Pipe Path 3
Pleasant Valley 24
Plantation Forest 26
Plantation House 20, 26
Police Station J
Portugee (Dutch) Battery 6
Post Office J
Potato Bay 12a
Pounceys 17
Powell's Battery 10
Powell's Bay 10
Powell's Valley 10
Power station 3
Prison J
Public Gardens J

Quarantine station 15

Redhill 17
Repulse Point 4
Roads, the James 4
Rock Mount 21
Rock Rose 10, 23
Rosemary Hall 15
Rosemary Plain 15
Ross, Mount 17
Run, the J, 2
Rupert's Ridge 2
Ruperts Valley 2, 3, 4

Saddle Battery 2, 3
St James' Church J
St Mark's Church 25
St Matthew's Church 22
St Matthew's Met Station 22
Sampsons Battery 2, 3
Sandy Bay Barn 10, 11, 20
Sandy Bay Basin 11, 18, 19, 20, 21, 23, 26
Sandy Bay Beach 12, 12a, 26
Sane Valley 26
Sarah's Valley 15
Scotland 18, 26
Seale's Battery 12a
Seale's Corner J
Sharks Valley 8, 9, 24
Sheep Pound 21
Shore Island 8
Sidepath 2
Signal stations 4, 5, 7, 26
Slave quarters 3, 15
Silver Hill 8, 24
Sister's Walk 2
Southern Ocean 13
South-west Point 20, 26
Speery Island 26
Spring Gut 18
Sugar Loaf 4, 7
Sugar Loaf Ridge 4

Teutonic Hall 22, 23, 24
Thompson's Bay 14
Thompson's Hill 18, 19
Thompson's Valley 14
Thompson's Wood 20, 26
Tobacco Plain 24, 25
Turks Cap 6, 7
Turks Cap Valley 5, 6

Verandah Quarters 1

Walbro Hall 24
Warrens Gut 8, 24
Water Gut 26
Waterwitch Monument 2
Wellington House J
White Gate 17
White Hill 11
Willowbank 26
Wranghams 23
Woody Ridge 21, 23, 24, 26

Youngs valley 26

People

Alexander family 19
Andrew, HRH Prince J, 16
Arnold, Dr J
Bahreini prisoners 1
Balcombe, Betsy 16, 24
Barnes, Major 16
Beatson, Governor 6
Benjamin, George 17, 20, 22
Bevian, Thomas 18
Blackmore, Governor 26
Black Oliver 7, 24
Boer prisoners 3, 5, 6, 15, 19, 26
Brooke, Thomas 11
Brookes, Mabel 16
Buddha J
Burchell, William 9, 25
Cason, Thomas 18
Chubb, Edward 2

Cockburn, Admiral 26
Darwin, Charles 5, 11
Deason Brothers 19
Des Fountain, John 21
Dinizulu 16
Doveton, Sir William 23
Dutch, the 3, 7, 15
Field, Governor 2
Francis, Henry 16
Gosse, Philip 1, 17
Greentree, Colonel 21
Halley, Edmund 22
Hancock, Richard 8
Hayward, E. 20
Heathcote, Ensign 24
Hooker, Sir Joseph 23
Jackson, E.L. 3
Janisch, Governor Hudson 24, 26
Janisch, William 2, 23
Jenkins, Governor 12a
Johnson, Lieutenant 19
Keigwin, Lieutenant 7
Lambert, Governor 12a
Lefroy, J.H. 25
Legg, John 26
London's Ben 5
Lowe, Governor Sir Hudson J, 23, 26
Lufkin, John 20
Malcolm, Admiral 16
Mashbone, Captain 1
Maskelyne, Neville 22
Massingham, Governor J
Mellis, G.W. 17
Mellis, J.C. 23
Munden, Sir Richard 2, 7
Mundy, Peter 13
Napoleon
– and the Barn 5
– and Admiral Cockburn 26
– and Mt Pleasant 23
– and Poppleton 10
– and Rock Rose 10
– and the Briars 16
– and Longwood 16, 25
– and Oaklands 26
– and Teutonic 23, 24
– and Willowbank 26
– Captivity 5, 21
– Death mask 5, 7
– Removal of body J
– Tomb 26
Patton, Governor 2, 10
Peel, Governor 16
Powell, Acting Governor 10
Powell, Gabriel 10
Pyke, Governor 7
Ross, Governor 17
Ross, James Clark 17, 23, 25
Rupert, Prince 3
Seale, R. 10
Slocum, Joshua 2
Sultan (slave) 21
Thornton, Tony 19, 26
Wellington, Duke of J, 16
'Yamstocks' 8

Plants

Agaves 3
Aloes 3
Arum lilies 18
Baby's toes 12
Bamboo 26
Bellflower, St Helena 23, 26
Boxwood 9
Cabbage trees 18, 23, 26
Cape gooseberries 24
Cape yew 18
Celery, wild 8
Cinchona 23
Coconuts 3
Coffee, St Helena 21
Dogwood, St Helena 23, 26
Ebony, St Helena 12a, 14, 20
Eucalyptus 24
Flax 21, 22, 23, 24
Ginger lily 8
Gorse 17
Gumwoods 6, 21, 25
Ice plants 12
Jellico 23
Kikuyu grass 17
Lemon trees 15
Lobelia, St Helena 23, 26
Loquats 21
Mesembryanthemum 5, 6, 7, 11, 12, 26
Norfolk Island pine 10, 23, 26
Old man salt bush 7
Olive, St Helena 22
Peepul trees J
Phormium tenax (see Flax)
Plantain, St Helena 20
Port Jackson willow 9
Prickly pear 1, 2, 3, 4, 14, 15
Samphire 1
Scrubwood 4, 9, 20, 25
Thorn trees (Kaffir Boom) 17, 18
Tomatoes, wild 12
Tree ferns 23, 26
Tungi (see Prickly pear)
Whitewood 23, 26
Wild mango 8
Yams 8

Birds

Canaries 9
Cardinal birds 23
Chukar partridge 14
Doves 17
Fairy terns 7, 21
Java sparrow 18
Moorhens 25
Noddy terns 26
Petrels 7, 20
Pheasants 22
Skuas 2
Sooty terns 20
Swainson's canary 9
Tropic birds 1, 26
Waxbills 19
Wirebird, the 5, 7

Miscellaneous

Basalt 9
Benguela Current 12
Camping J, 8, 10, 12, 23
Cannon 2, 4
Cavalley 4
Caves 12, 12a, 15
Cricket 5, 16
Crown Waste 13
Dennison Rebellion 8, 20
Diplomatic Wireless Service 7, 25
Dolphin (ship) J
Dolphins 14
Dugongs 13
Dykes 5, 6, 7, 20
Earwig 25
East India Company J, 4
Elephant seals 13

Erosion 5, 6, 8, 9, 20, 25
Fortified Lines 3
Goats 5, 11
Gold 1
Great Fire of London 21
Gypsum 7
Heritage Society 4
Jack (fish) 4
Jackson mutiny 19
Lime kiln 12, 12a
Manatees 13
Papanui J
Phonolite 9, 26
Records, the St Helena 3
Rock falls J, 2
Sea cows 13
Sharks In, 8, 26
Solomons J, 18, 19, 21, 24, 26
Spring lines/springs 2, 8, 22
Swimming In, 1, 4, 7, 8, 12, 13, 14, 15
Trachyte 9
Tuff 2
Volcanoes 4
Walled Up Valleys 1, 4, 12a
Waste Stabilization Ponds 1
Wave-cut platform 7, 12, 12a, 13
White sand deposits 12
Wyndham, HMS 1